GOD STORIES

GOD STORIES

Inspiring Encounters with

the Divine

Edited by

JENNIFER SKIFF

Harmony Books
New York

Copyright © 2008 by Jennifer Skiff

All rights reserved.
Published in the United States by Harmony Books, an imprint of the
Crown Publishing Group, a division of Random House, Inc., New York.
www.crownpublishing.com

HARMONY BOOKS is a registered trademark and the Harmony Books
colophon is a trademark of Random House, Inc.

Library of Congress Cataloging-in-Publication Data

First Edition
Skiff, Jennifer, 1961–
God stories : inspiring encounters with the divine / Jennifer Skiff.—
1st ed.
1. Miracles—Anecdotes.   2. Presence of God—Anecdotes.   I. Title.
BL487.S55 2008
204'.32—dc22   2007051750

ISBN 978-0-307-38268-9

Printed in the United States of America

Design by Lauren Dong

10 9 8 7 6 5

To all the beautiful souls who have passed through
this life and remain with me today

Contents

GOD STORIES

Introduction

Why am I here? Is there more? Does God exist? These questions nag at us incessantly throughout our lives. But the answers are elusive, always just out of reach. Today we are fact-driven people: we need evidence before we form opinions and often dismiss events that can't be logically explained. Yet we desperately want the security that comes with having a certain future. The search for that security has divided people into two camps: those who look for solace in organized religion and its promise of an afterlife, and those who consider themselves spiritual but not religious—they believe their souls are going somewhere, but they're not sure exactly where. Regardless of what camp you're in, we all want the same thing. We want confirmation that what we believe is true. We want proof of modern-day encounters with the Divine.

I've been offered proof of God's existence at regular intervals in my life through experiences so profound they've given goose bumps to atheists. These epiphanies have blanketed me with an inner peace, washing away my fears and giving me hope for the future. The intense joy I feel at these times eventually dissipates and I drift into a safe complacency. As time passes and life events take their toll, I start to question again until yet another unexpected collision with the Divine awakens me like a plunge into cold water and replenishes my faith. I know I'm not alone. Because the proof we're given is not tangible, it's often held tightly for a short time and then released. But our appetite remains insatiable. Like ants to a grain of sugar, we crave more. And that's what has brought us here.

As you turn the pages in this book, a chill may overwhelm you, your eyes may fill with tears, and the hair on your arms may suddenly stand as the answers to the questions you've always wanted to know become apparent.

My reason for writing a book of this nature is not the obvious one. I'm certainly not an expert on the subject of God or religion. The idea first came to me when a minister asked if I had any "God Stories." I asked her what she meant, and she explained that a God Story was a miracle-like experience that proves God exists.

No one had ever asked me that question before. I did have stories. I hadn't dared to tell many people about them, but I definitely had had what I believed to be encounters with the Divine. The concept piqued my interest as a journalist, and I wondered if many other people had stories too. To find out, I began to poll my friends, and what happened next surprised me most. I realized that a Divine intelligence that many call God is connecting with millions of people every day.

One of my own encounters happened when I was thirty-two years old. It was a time of overwhelming sadness and disappointment. Professionally I was thriving—working as a correspondent for CNN, the biggest news network in the world. But personally I was very unhappy and felt like a failure. I was married for the second time, and for the second time I was planning to divorce.

It was at this time that I began experiencing a debilitating pain in my right leg. After months of consultations with doctors who couldn't determine what was wrong, I was sent to the chief of orthopedics at Massachusetts General Hospital in Boston, where it was confirmed that I had a tumor in my bone marrow. I needed to be operated on immediately.

When I awoke from surgery, my doctor told me he had been able to save my leg temporarily, but I did in fact have bone cancer. And although it sounds terrible, I felt a sense of relief knowing I would no longer have to continue on with my life.

And then something strange happened. Within forty-eight hours of my diagnosis, I began receiving cards, flowers, stuffed animals, and gifts of delicious things to eat. I had no idea how so many people had learned I was in the hospital. A person I hadn't seen since I was a young girl wrote to tell me how I had influenced her life. Notes arrived from different parts of the country from people I didn't know telling me they were praying for me. My friends and family cried and overwhelmed me with their affection. I was engulfed by a warm blanket of love.

Nearly a week after the surgery, I was in my hospital bed envisioning my funeral when my doctor rushed into my room, breathless. He looked at me and smiled a big, wide smile.

"I never get to say this," he said, shaking his head and throwing his hands into the air. "Benign!"

"Benign? What do you mean, 'benign'? I thought it was malignant."

"It was," he said. "The slide we looked at told us it was malignant. The lab results have just come back, and they say it's benign. We're going with benign!"

The entire experience was all the proof I needed. I had been given signs before, but this was obvious. There was a God for me, one who made it clear it was important I continue on with my life—to work toward positive change in the world and to see and understand all I had been blessed with.

Some people spend their whole lives questioning, while others are offered what they believe is proof. The confirmation for actress Jane Seymour came while she was filming a movie in Spain. She was given antibiotics for a bronchitis infection and immediately went into anaphylactic shock. "The next thing I remember, I was panicking and then I wasn't panicking," she said. "I was very calm. I was looking down at my body. Then I realized that I was out of my body and that I was going to die. So I asked whoever was up there—God, a Higher Power, whatever one wants to call it—I just said, 'Whoever you are, I will never deny your existence. I will never let you down. I'm not going to waste one minute of my life if I have it back.'" In this book you'll find out what happened next that changed Jane Seymour's life forever.

God Stories is a collection of such *Aha!* experiences. The stories are told by people from every walk of life—all celebrating that breakthrough moment when they received dramatic confirmation of the existence of a Divine Power. The result is pure inspiration: a compilation of extraordinary experiences that have renewed spirits and affirmed faiths.

In California, Senator Dick Mountjoy's spiritual awakening came at a time when he was embroiled in a political battle and in the depths of professional despair. A stranger approached him, put her hand on his shoulder, and asked if she could pray for him. His life changed in that instant. He describes how a warm feeling quickly spread throughout his body and a sense of calm fell over him. From that moment on, he felt a continuous sense of comfort and all his worries slipped away.

In Maine, a young mother describes the chilling moment she realized that she and her children were going to die. She was driving down a country road when two drag racers came over a hill directly in front of her, taking both lanes. She didn't have time to avoid a head-on collision. In *God Stories*, she tells how God intervened and saved her life.

Shirley Blake describes a brutal rape as her epiphany. She was fifty-nine years old. In what can only be described as the most frightening moment in her life, she says she heard God's voice reassure and comfort her. In this book you find out why, today, she says the experience was enlightening.

I realized the significance of this project when I started collecting stories. My goal was to be interviewed by the media in hopes that the publicity would direct people to my website, where they could submit their stories. At the beginning of this process, I was interviewed by a newspaper editor in his office. When he wrapped up his questions, I asked him if he had a story. He did, and as he told it, he cried. I was completely taken aback and didn't know what to do. And then, as I listened, I realized how privileged I was that he was sharing his story with me.

Little did I know that this profound experience would be repeated every day from then on. As the sun rose each morning, I found myself hopping out of bed and rushing to my computer to read the incoming stories. Some brought me to tears. Others simply surprised me, like the one my husband unexpectedly shared about the scar on his forehead.

When I began the search for stories, I said I was looking for one thing: the moment a person received personal proof that God or a Divine Power exists. People of many religions, cultures, and races responded. The stories they provided are true to them. There will be skepticism in response to this book, and I think it makes for a healthy dialogue.

I started the collection process by setting up a website, www.GodStories.com, where people could submit their stories. I then worked with the media to direct people there. At GodStories.com they were asked to provide personal details, declare that the stories were their own, and agree to their names' being used. Those who were not willing to verify their credibility by using their own names were not considered for publication.

If I thought the story was right for the book, I contacted the person and often began a series of interviews via e-mail and over the phone. I was not always able to conduct in-person interviews, because the stories came in from all over the world. After the interviews, some stories were no longer considered, for various reasons.

Surprisingly, as the stories came in, similar themes emerged. These themes became chapters, and the book you are holding took shape.

I suspect your life will be changed by reading this book just as mine was after hearing these stories. I have been left with a sense of amazement and optimism as well as an abiding belief in something I once questioned. And it doesn't stop on the last page, because once you give yourself permission to believe, you'll find God Stories happening in your life every day.

"A BEAUTIFUL SIGN"

Looking Beyond

"God, please give me the words to say!"

MARIAN BROWN, *Court Reporter*

As an adult, I drifted away from the Roman Catholic faith in which I was raised. I still believed in God and prayed on my own but was often skeptical that he was listening. His message on one special day wiped away all doubt.

My husband, Steve, and I lived with our two sons in San Diego County, California. Our home was the first to burn in what is known as the Firestorm of 2003—the second-largest wildfire in U.S. history. It burned over 700,000 acres, destroying wildlife and 3,640 homes, and taking 15 lives in October of that year.

It would be several days after evacuating before we could return to the ruins of our home. A group of twenty of our closest friends spent all morning going through the ashes with shovels to see if there was anything salvageable before our lot was cleared for rebuilding. Their efforts were unsuccessful. There was absolutely nothing left; in fact, the fire was so hot that there were holes in the ground where trees had burned to their roots.

I decided to bring our two sons to the site later that morning. I wasn't sure how they would react, but I knew they needed to see it with their own eyes in order to begin the healing process. My older son, Evan, was thirteen years old at the time and was very stoic. It was my younger son, ten-year-old Erik, who broke my heart as he walked through the ashes quietly wiping away tears.

I didn't know what to say or do when my children looked

imploringly to me, yet I knew that my reaction would be key to how they handled this disaster. I began to pray as I stood there: "God, please help me. Give me the words. What do I say to my children, who have lost the only home they've ever known, lost everything they have in the world?" At that very moment, Erik called out, "Hey, you guys missed something. There's a book over here." Our friends said, "No way. We've been sifting through the ashes for four and a half hours and there's nothing left, certainly nothing made of paper." But Erik insisted until we finally all trudged over to where he was pointing at the remains of a book. He bent over and picked up the book, and as he did, the layers of pages fell away, disintegrating in his hand.

Everyone shook their heads and began walking away. Someone said, "Oh, we're so sorry, honey. There's nothing left but ashes."

"No. Wait. Look," Erik said, extending his arm. There in the palm of his hand was the most fragile piece of ash, the size of a half-dollar. On it was a picture of a family holding hands and three words: COUNT YOUR BLESSINGS.

"I would love to see this little boy's face"

PAUL HAMMOND, *Network Administrator*

My wife and I had been sending shoe boxes of presents for Operation Christmas Child for a few years. One year we had packed a really nice box for a young boy. As we finished packing, I looked at my wife and said, "I would love to see this little boy's face when he opens this box."

The following year we were preparing to do another box and happened to pick up a publication for Operation Christmas Child. My wife was reading it when she called me over to look at something. There, on the bottom of page three, was a picture of a little boy hugging a teddy bear he had just received in his Christmas box. Lo and behold, on closer examination of the box in front of him, we saw all the unique items (and wrapping) we'd chosen the previous year, including the very recognizable bear. It was our box!

"Mom, look!"

BARBARA EIKOST,
Retired Hospice Volunteers Director

I have always trusted my faith but had never experienced a "spiritual event" until the morning of January 5, 1998. My sixty-one-year-old husband, Bill, had gone to the hospital on New Year's Eve when his multiple myeloma symptoms worsened. For the next four days he seemed to stabilize, but we realized the treatment that had worked for seven years was no longer effective.

Our son who lived nearby had been very attentive, and on Sunday the fourth, our other son in Atlanta hopped a plane for Toledo because he sensed his presence was important. Bill was delighted to have his boys with him. He was lucid, mindful of the Rose Bowl results, and seemed peaceful as friends stopped in to wish him well. My sons and I went home in the late evening.

We were awakened suddenly at 4 a.m. with a call from the hospital saying that Bill was experiencing difficulty and was asking for us. We were at his bedside in fifteen minutes. He was in great distress, trying to get oxygen and struggling to live. Our physician was present, helping us to understand what was happening.

My sons and I surrounded Bill with passionate expressions of our love and gratitude for all he had meant to us. Just as he breathed his last breath, my son literally shouted, "Mom, look!" Right outside my husband's large hospital window on that gray January day was a vivid rainbow! There was neither rain nor sun, but this ribbon of color in the sky told us in ways that defy explanation that our beloved husband and father was being escorted from this world to a better place.

I have never questioned this experience, and I have never expected to fully understand it. I simply accept it as a remarkable expression of the gracious mystery.

"God truly saved me"

STEPHEN WOOD, Nursery Owner

It was October 28, 1991, and I had decided to go paragliding from a three-hundred-foot ridge. It was a particularly windy day, and when I reached the ridge, I felt it was too dangerous to soar from the top. So I walked two-thirds of the way down in hopes of doing a small glide from there. I had put down my bag and was adjusting one of my risers (straps similar to a seat belt that help with balance) when I heard a rustling in the bushes. I had been warned that there were quite a few poisonous snakes on the property, and immediately I thought it might be a snake. So I grabbed my bag, threw it over my shoulder, did a safety check of both risers, and jumped. But the moment I jumped, I realized I hadn't adjusted the second riser—I was totally out of sync. I spun into the ridge, corrected myself, and then got caught in the updraft. Now I was six hundred feet above where I had started. Severe turbulence then caused the paraglider to deflate and collapse. Like a sack of potatoes, I fell more than three hundred feet to the ground.

My back was broken, but I was alive. When I came out of intensive care, doctors told me the accident had caused so much damage that my spine would have to be fused together with plates and bolts. I had a burst vertebra, and two others were fractured. The operation would take place in three days.

The morning before the operation, I awoke to see a vision of a doctor in a white coat standing by the side of my bed. He was in a happy mood and told me not to have the operation but to lie in bed and let my spine heal naturally. He went on to say that he'd had a patient who had suffered a similar injury to mine in a parachute accident and had let his spine heal naturally, lying still for eight weeks, and he was fine. I thanked him and put my hand out to shake his, but he literally disappeared—evaporated before me. But he had been as real as any person!

A nurse came into my room five minutes later and I told her what had happened. She told me to do exactly what he had advised and to tell no one of my experience. Later that morning, I was being wheeled out in my bed to have an MRI body scan and recognized the doctor in a life-size portrait on the wall in the corridor. On my return, I told the nurse and she said she knew. The man, she said, was Sir George Bedbrook, a greatly admired and respected surgeon whom the ward was named after. His specialty was spinal healing using natural, nonsurgical methods. The nurse then told me he had passed away seven years before.

That was a hard day. I had to tell my surgeon, wife, and parents that I was going to lie in bed and let my spine heal naturally. The surgeon explained that the injury was much too severe for this option. My wife and parents were left with the job of convincing me to go ahead with the operation.

I didn't go ahead with it, and today, fifteen years later, I am in perfect health and run a very physically demanding business. I have never forgotten my visit, which was truly an act of divine intervention direct from God. I consider myself the luckiest person in the world!

"You can do it!"

MARIE DESJARDINS, *Retired Waitress*

When I was twenty-eight years old, in 1978, my small intestine ruptured. My six-year-old daughter found me on the floor of our home, unconscious. She called for help and I was rushed to the hospital, but it was too late. The doctor didn't think I was going to make it. My body was shutting down and I was drifting in and out of consciousness. The doctor called family members and the priest to give me the last rites.

That same night I was alone in my hospital room and suffering from excruciating pain when a nurse appeared beside me. She was dressed in uniform and seemed to be very old, with many wrinkles in her face. I looked at her hands. They were stretched out toward me. Something inside me made me feel that if I touched those hands, my pain would be less severe. So I reached out for them, but she disappeared.

I remember telling other nurses about the woman, but they all said there was no one of that description who worked there. I told the doctor, and he said I was hallucinating. I then told my priest, and he said it was the Blessed Mother coming for me. But, he added, she didn't take me because I had something else to do before going.

Despite the odds, I did survive. But when I recounted the story of the Blessed Mother to my husband, he actually thought I was going crazy. And so I stopped telling the story and didn't mention it again.

Twenty years later I saw a notice on a church bulletin board for a pilgrimage to a village in Bosnia-Herzegovina called Medjugorje. I had never heard of the place before and didn't know of its importance. As I read about it, I found out that it was a small village where the Blessed Virgin Mary had been appearing and giving messages to the world. I knew I needed to go.

And so I went, traveling all the way from my home in northern Maine to Bosnia-Herzegovina. When I got there, I knelt to pray before the statue of Mary. Her hands were outstretched to me, and in that instant I was reminded of the woman who had appeared to me twenty years before as I was dying in the hospital. They were the same hands! As I looked at the fingers on the hands, I noticed they were all black and chipped, and I found myself saying, "Blessed Mother, if I only lived close to you, I would fix and paint your hands." I don't know why I said it. I had never held a paintbrush! But as I was saying it, I heard an inner voice in my heart telling me that I would do it.

Shortly after I returned home, a man I knew only as an acquaintance knocked on the door of my house. He had never been there before. He asked me only one question. He wanted to know where he could get a pair of hands fixed on a statue he had of Our Lady of Grace. I couldn't believe it. Why had he come to me? I found myself telling him that I could do it even though I had no idea how! But I kept hearing an inner voice in my heart saying, "You can do it. You can do it."

That night I prayed for help to fix the hands. The next day I went to Wal-Mart and bought plaster of paris and Play-Doh. I worked with the different compounds all week, sculpting and cooking them in my oven until I got it right.

Eventually I taught myself how to fix a statue using joint cement and fine sandpaper, finishing up with paint. I have now fixed and renovated more than a thousand statues of Our Lady. I have never charged anyone for it. This is my mission. This is my purpose. I think this is my ministry.

I kept silent about this story for twenty years because I thought people would think I was crazy. But I do feel I was kept alive that night when I was twenty-eight years old to do this work.

"Elvis was my way of reconnecting with her"

BILL BUTLER, *Radio Broadcaster*

My mother passed away when I was six years old. She was a single mother and had been raising me by herself. She was all I had.

My mom was a huge Elvis fan. Listening to Elvis records with her is one of my most cherished memories. After she passed, Elvis was my way of reconnecting with her.

When I was twenty-six years old, my wife and I had the chance to go to Nashville. I made her promise that we would end the week in Memphis. I wanted to see Graceland.

The tour was great, and we had a fantastic time. There is a gift shop at each of the museum exits at Graceland, tempting you to buy something as you leave. I picked up a DVD at the first shop and was determined to stop spending money and just breeze through the other shops on the way out.

After leaving the Sincerely Elvis Museum, I was walking swiftly out of the gift shop when a shiny little object caught my eye. There were hundreds of name pendants on display, and the one that caught my eye was out of alphabetical order. It was heart shaped with a silhouette of Elvis and my mother's name, Sheila.

At that moment I felt a shiver throughout my body. I believe that my heart was reaching out to God, asking for confirmation that my mother was in a better place, and he felt compelled to answer. At that moment I knew there was a God and that I was loved. I have never doubted since.

"Believe"

BILL FOLEY, *Retired Teacher*

I planned on visiting my brother on December 29, 2002, in an ongoing effort to mend our relationship. I thought we could watch the New England Patriots' last game of the year together. It turned out to be a very cold day, though, and I didn't feel like leaving my warm home. My conscience pricked me to go—reminding me that I would enjoy the game more if I watched it with someone else. But I didn't go.

At the time, I had serious doubts that God existed. Friends had suggested inviting God into everyday situations to try to make contact with him. So, instead of watching the game with my brother, I invited God to watch the game with me.

It was a low-scoring game. The Miami Dolphins led by only eight points but had dominated. With just eight minutes to play, the Patriots' quarterback attempted a pass that was intercepted. It looked as if the game was over. The television cameras focused on the fans streaming out of the stadium.

I turned to God and reminded him that I still struggled with a belief in his existence. And although I wasn't really concerned with the outcome of the game, I humbly assured him that if he were to engineer a turnaround at this point, it would strengthen my rather weak faith.

The next drive stalled on the ten-yard line and the opponents settled for a field goal, extending their lead to eleven points, which would require the Patriots to score twice in five minutes in order to win.

The Patriots then received the opponent's kickoff, but a couple of plays later, the quarterback threw the ball into an opponent's arms. Sensing disaster, a Patriots player blatantly interfered to avoid the interception. I waited for the officials to penalize him, but, strangely, they ruled that the opponents had done the interfering and gave the ball to the Patriots. It was then that I asked God if he had distorted the officials' perception at the time of the infraction. He didn't respond, but in the next few minutes it seemed a switch had been thrown. The New England team suddenly was alive. Then came, in addition to the previous blatantly erroneous call, two other questionable rulings by officials, two disastrous kicks by the Dolphins, two circus catches by Patriot receivers, and a favorable coin toss. The kickoff was so unusual that one of the players told a reporter, "It was as if the Lord reached down and touched the ball to say, 'I'm with you guys!' "

During that mind-boggling few minutes, I found myself asking God, "How do you do this?" I had a sense that there was a different connection to my mind, something I had never experienced before.

But then the old familiar thoughts that I have always identified as my own began: "Be serious—you've seen these things happen plenty of times. It was all just a coincidence."

The Patriots won the game by a field goal in overtime. I couldn't believe it! I had asked for it to happen and it did. I ended up on my knees in front of the TV. "I can't believe you did that. You're really real," I thought. The TV was still on, but the audio was off. I saw the quarterback being interviewed and then the start of an ad for Guinness beer. The storm continued in my mind. "You've seen this sort of thing a hundred times. It's a coincidence. You're deluding yourself!" Doubt crept back in. The ending of the Guinness ad faded to black and then one word filled the screen: BELIEVE. I laughed and cried and I've never been the same since.

"A framed picture of Christ"

PATRICIA FRYTERS, *Administrative Clerk*

I t was 5 p.m. and the sun was setting early. My Catholic church was open for Adoration of the Blessed Sacrament, and I was sitting in a corner pew, spending an hour with Jesus just before Easter.

A friend of mine got up to leave, and my eyes followed him across the church pews until I saw on a wall a framed picture of Christ—just his face, looking down with a crown of thorns around his head. He had blood dripping from his left temple, and his head was resting on two gold bars of the sun's rays. I gazed for a while, thinking about how beautiful the rays of light were.

The image on the picture interested me so much that I decided to have another look at it on my way out. I walked over to where it hung and, much to my surprise, what I saw wasn't there. Instead, there was a big framed cross-stitch of a sacrificial lamb caught in a thornbush! I said to myself, "What happened?"

It didn't really strike me until I got home, and then it dawned on me: I had received a miracle from Christ, a direct message. The Lord was telling me that he was the sacrificial lamb!

Every Sunday I still pass that framed picture, and I smile to myself.

"Faith"

KATHY CAIRNS, *Medical Assistant*

It was the morning of my son's wedding. The ceremony was going to be held in the backyard of our home, but the weather was horrible. The rain was coming down so hard that the tent was collapsing as my husband and friends tried to put it up.

I got into the shower and started praying to the Blessed Mother. I prayed for the rain to stop and the sun to come out.

As I stepped out of the shower, my husband asked if I had written something on the fog-covered window on the opposite side of the bathroom. I said, "No. What do you mean?" We both looked at the window at the same time and read the letters. They spelled out FAITH!

I knew then that if I put my trust in the Lord, everything would turn out okay. And at that moment a calm came over me.

Everything did turn out okay. We had the wedding inside. It was a beautiful and intimate ceremony, one that our friends and family will always remember.

"Let go, let God"

SUSAN MOORE, *Pet Sitter*

I was attending a recovery group through my church, and the counselor suggested that to free ourselves, we visualize placing a box of our troubles on the altar before God, asking him to accept our burden.

I decided to modify that suggestion. I wrote down all the people I wanted to forgive and be forgiven by, all the ills I wanted to release, and all the sins I wanted to confess. I then put this paper into a gold box along with pictures of my ex-husband and the dream home that we had built together and that I had lost in the divorce. I then took the box to a local church. On the hill in front of the church are three crosses. I went up the hill and buried the box beneath the center cross. Before I left, I placed my hand on the cross and asked God to accept my burdens, as they were too big for me to handle on my own. I repeated the words "Let go, let God" over and over again as I began walking to my car.

Halfway back, I turned around to see that the clouds had parted over the center cross and sunbeams were shining down directly over my offering. It was truly the most awesome sight of my life!

When I reached the car and saw the clouds had closed, I knew my burdens had been accepted by God, and I had peace in my life for the first time in a very long time.

"I was praying and weeping for these people"

RHONDA GILLAM, *Friend*

My best friend is Betty Cuthbert, the Australian Olympic runner who broke sixteen world records in her career and who is the only woman in the world to win the 100-, 200-, and 400-meter races in the Olympics.

In November 2004, Betty was asked to give her name to the plight of forty-five Vietnamese people who were imprisoned in a detention facility on Christmas Island, Australia. They had escaped Vietnam by boat after the government began torturing and imprisoning many of them for handing out pro-democracy and freedom-of-religion brochures. They had made it to Australia, seeking asylum, but it hadn't been granted. When Betty was asked to help, they had been locked up for three years.

Betty was now in a wheelchair, suffering from multiple sclerosis. She was paralyzed, with the exception of one hand. But after hearing the story of these people who had fled their country in fear and had still not been permitted entry into Australia, we decided to go and meet them.

The conditions were pretty stark—just dirt and shaded meeting areas. A barbed-wire fence outlined the perimeter, with guards at the gate and inside. These people, these beautiful, gentle people, met us with the only gift they could give—vegetables and sunflowers they had grown.

After we met with the refugees, our driver took us on a tour of the island. He stopped at a magnificent casino complex that was closed for political reasons. I got out to walk the grounds and found myself thinking about the people I had just left. I couldn't stop crying, thinking of the detainees and how they were imprisoned. Here I was, walking around the abandoned gardens of a multi-million-dollar complex. I kept thinking about how those people could be free and tending these gardens.

As I wept, I found myself saying to the Lord, "Why is this? Why are they detained when they could be looking after this place?" All of a sudden, and it's hard to describe, I found myself physically turned around and walking four steps in the other direction. I stopped at the spot where two tree limbs had fallen over each other to form the most perfect cross. At that second, in my heart I heard, "Rhonda, the cross is empty, but I am with you both."

The Vietnamese people were freed twelve months after our trip. Betty's presence at the facility generated the press attention and subsequent public awareness that helped to free them.

"G.O.D."

BRIGITTE CARNEVALE, *Administrative Assistant*

I was having a horrible morning. It was snowing, and I didn't feel well. My husband had a terrible pain in his leg and couldn't walk. I felt I needed to get him to the hospital, but he said to leave him at home. I was late for work, and I still had to get my three-year-old to day care. Nothing was going right.

As I drove to work, I was very distressed and I was talking out loud to God. I remember passing a church and saying, "Can't you just talk to me?" I almost drove off the road when I noticed the perfect letters above the church in the clouds. The letters spelled out G.O.D.

The vision was so startling but felt so comforting. He did speak to me.

"A beautiful sign"

MICHELLE BIAGI, Mom

The day of my father's funeral was a nasty, gloomy day. I was on the way to the service when I saw a rainbow, and I said, "Okay, Dad, the cancer is gone now and you're with God because he's giving us this beautiful sign that you're okay." And as I said it, a feeling of comfort washed over me.

But I wasn't the only one to receive comfort from that rainbow. My family and even the priest mentioned it. In the church, the priest talked about how the rainbow was a sign from God that my dad was in heaven, out of pain and in God's loving arms. A friend in Montana (we live in Ohio) told us that on the day of the funeral, there wasn't a cloud in the sky, but there was a rainbow outside her door.

The rainbows continued throughout the week, and ever since then, when I'm feeling stressed or going through difficult times, a rainbow always appears to reassure me that both my dad and God are guiding me.

The examples are endless but are often at important moments in my life. The first Thanksgiving I ever hosted for the family, I was deep-frying the turkey in the backyard when I saw a rainbow. I felt it was a message from Dad that he was with me on Thanksgiving. On Easter morning I woke to see a gorgeous double rainbow in the western sky. I woke my mom to show her, and we began our Easter in a very special way. Recently, I was having a trying week with my two-year-old when I saw a beautiful rainbow.

And even more recently, while visiting Vietnam, my husband's cousin became sick with the Asian bird flu and tragically died. I had been thinking about her and praying for her family when I realized that on the day she died, I had seen a rainbow. I immediately broke into tears at the awesome power of God's presence and his reminder that he is there and our loved ones are with him. It's all a sign for me. I know that there's a heaven and that there's life after death, and that sometime I'll see my dad again.

"It was almost an exclamation point from the heavens"

DAVE KREMNITZER, *Letter Carrier*

Numbers have always had a special meaning for me.

June 2002 was a sad time. Jan, a dear friend of mine and my wife's best friend, suffered a heart attack and died. I was asked to give a eulogy at her funeral, and immediately the number three came into my head.

Jan's funeral took place three days after her death. During my eulogy I noted that she had passed away on June 3, 2002. I recalled fond memories of weddings, shared vacations, and special events together. She had two wonderful families of three. There was Jan, her husband, and her son. And there was Jan, her brother, and her father. Both families of three became two with her death.

As I finished the eulogy, I looked upward. The sky was completely overcast except for a patch of blue above me. At that very moment, the patch broke into a perfect number three. It was as if God was talking directly to me. If there was any doubt that somebody above was listening, that really dispelled it right there. Not only had God listened to me, but he had spiritually energized my life forever. It was almost an exclamation point from the heavens.

"IT'S ALL GOOD NEWS"

Listening to the Voice

"Turn around!"

LUIS MUÑOZ, *Executive Television Producer*

It was a stormy Texas night and I was out way too late, about 1:15 in the morning. I was driving home from my girlfriend's house. As I blasted my radio, trying to keep awake, I noticed a black truck speeding toward me on the other side of the highway. From across the median, I could see that the driver was losing control. The truck started swerving all over the road. As I began to pass it going the opposite way, it crashed violently into the median, spraying glass across my car.

The truck finally came to a stop a few yards farther down the highway. Smoke was coming from it. I drove as fast and as safely as I could to the nearest exit and turned around. It must have taken me one minute, and by the time I reached the wreck and parked on the side of the road, a man and a woman were already helping the truck driver. They were off-duty emergency medical service technicians, and the driver was obviously drunk. He smelled of alcohol and there were empty beer cans inside the truck. The medics began trying to wake him while I held his hand and talked to him.

We had been there about five minutes, freezing and wet, when I stepped back to see the whole picture. I was shaking from the cold. It was then that I heard a voice say, "Turn around!" It was loud and eerie, in my head. As I turned, I saw a small white Honda heading full-speed toward us all—skidding across the wet road. I had less than a second to turn, yell at the others, and jump out of the way. As I and the other two people were in the air, the Honda ran straight into the truck, injuring the truck driver even more, severing his leg.

The female medic and I landed on the other side of the road and barely avoided being run over by oncoming cars. The male medic hadn't been able to jump as far and was knocked out but ended up being okay. Neither of them had heard anything, not the voice or the car. They both looked at me and said, "Thank you! Thank you! Thank you!"

People who had stopped for the first accident on the opposite side of the road swore they had not seen the out-of-control car coming, and when it hit, they thought we had all been smashed. A teen who witnessed it ran over to me and said, "Dude, how did y'all move so fast?"

We were all shaking, disturbed, and thankful. None of us fully understood what had just taken place. We were all sure of one thing: something or someone had helped us—no doubt about it!

"Stop!"

KELLY NEWTON WORDSWORTH,
Singer/Songwriter

I had been searching for God since I was a child. I had been on an intense journey of doing personal growth–style workshops and was very into the New Age movement. While reading a book by Eileen Caddy, one of the founders of the Findhorn Foundation, I stopped at one sentence that changed my life: "Jesus said if we would obey God that we could do what he did and even greater things."

Immediately after reading that sentence I got up and walked outside, down to a place that I call the fairy glen, and I looked up in the sky and said to God, "I give you my whole life to serve you and make a difference for you on this earth. I ask that you tell me what to do, and I want to do what Jesus said."

The next day I went jogging in the Australian bush. As I ran, I found myself in a completely euphoric state, enjoying the beauty of nature around me and watching the sunlight sparkle on the trees. And then, out of the blue, a man's voice called, "Stop!" with such force that I stopped on the spot. I looked around for a person and there was no one there. And then I looked down on the ground. If I hadn't stopped exactly in the spot I did, my foot would have landed straight in front of a deadly poisonous seven-foot dugite snake's mouth. I would have been killed.

The extraordinary thing was that there was no fear in me. I knew that God had just saved my life. He was real. He had shouted at me with a real voice.

"Meg"

MEG ROBINSON, *Teacher*

I was driving home late at night on the interstate in Vermont when I started to fall asleep. I was roused by a deep male voice coming from behind my right shoulder. The voice simply called my first name sternly: "Meg!" I felt as if the voice were familiar, but I couldn't quite place it. I pulled over and rolled down my window as I realized what had just happened. It was a really weird feeling. I felt as if someone very familiar who knew me really well had just saved me from crashing.

I still struggle with believing in God, but the memory of this simple event comforts me.

"Put your leg out!"

RICHARD ABEL,
Roofing and Siding Business Owner

It was 1975. I was twenty-one years old and working on a roofing crew in Hershey, Pennsylvania. The job site was a two-story home that was separated from a neighbor's property by a spiked iron fence. Normally, when you put a ladder against a house, it should be on flat, solid ground. But the fence and its close proximity to the house prevented us from positioning the ladder correctly. We were forced to put it at nearly a ninety-degree incline (first mistake), and both feet of the ladder weren't solidly placed on the ground (second mistake).

All of us were up and down the ladder most of the day until my final ascent in the afternoon. I was nearing the top roofline when, in an instant, one side rail of the ladder lost contact with the ground and the ladder flipped sideways. So now, instead of the ladder being face-on against the house, it was side-on, and I was falling backward with both my hands holding the ladder in a death grip.

As I fell, a vision went through my mind of being impaled on the spiked fence below. And then a calm male voice called out in my head and said, "Put your leg out." In that fraction of a second, I argued that putting my leg outward would only serve to kick me away from the house. Loudly, like a stern father, the voice demanded, "Put your leg out!" I put my leg out and it touched the side of the house, somehow stopping the ladder from falling. I don't know how, but my leg suspended the fall for just enough time for the crew to save me.

No one can take this experience away from me. I am now fifty-two years old. I am married with two children and have a healthy fear of heights. To this day, I cannot explain why that ladder stopped its slide and saved me from certain death. But I do feel that the loud, instructional voice was my guardian angel, and through God's intervention, it was not my time—he had bigger plans for me in my life's journey. I thank him daily for my wife (whom I met shortly afterward) and the two children whom but for him I never would have known.

"Everything is going to be all right"

KERRI SCHUH, *Bookkeeper*

Twenty years ago, as I was giving birth to my daughter, I began to hemorrhage and lost consciousness during the delivery. When I came to, I was in the recovery room. My husband was sitting next to me in a rocking chair, holding our newborn daughter. He gave her to me to hold, but I quickly asked him to take her because I could feel I was losing consciousness again.

This time while I was unconscious, I had the clear impression that God was with me. He was telling me not to worry, that everything was going to be all right. I would not die, but I would have to have a hysterectomy. And then the feeling of his presence was gone.

I drifted in and out of consciousness as doctors and nurses were working on me. I wanted to tell them that God said I needed to have a hysterectomy, but I couldn't talk. Finally, my doctor came to my bedside and told me I was going to need a hysterectomy. I was able to whisper, "Yes, I know. Just hurry."

Whenever I tell this story to someone, although they don't come out and say it, I get the impression that they think I was just dreaming. But I am convinced that God was really talking to me. I vividly remember God telling me what was going to happen as vividly as I remember trying to tell the doctors I needed to have a hysterectomy.

"Slow down now!"

KATHY SHIELDS, *Cottage Manager*

I had always believed in God but had reached a point in my life where I didn't feel I needed to go to church anymore. I really didn't feel I needed God's guidance to be a good wife and mother—until something happened that changed my mind.

One day my son asked, "Mom, can Mark come over to play after school today?" Without hesitation I responded, "You know, Alex, having someone come over to play is a big responsibility." I couldn't believe my own ears. Why would I say such a thing? I loved to have my son's friends over to play. Again, he asked, "Mom, can Mark come over to play?" This time I said, "Yes, of course you can have Mark come over to play this afternoon." And then he asked, "Mom, can you bring Mark home today after we play?" Without hesitation I responded, "You know, Alex, bringing children home after school is a tremendous responsibility." I was temporarily aghast at my response. Frustrated by my own words, I came to my senses and said, "Yes, of course I will."

Mark and Alex had a wonderful afternoon playing together, but when it was time for Mark to go home, I hesitated and questioned whether I should leave my own children alone while I took Mark home. It was an absurd thought and one I had never entertained before—leaving my children alone. And so I packed them all into the car.

As I turned onto the main road, a voice—the same voice that had been talking to me all day—yelled at me, "Slow down *now!*" I immediately took my foot off the accelerator and looked up. Two cars were drag racing—using both lanes—and were heading straight for us. I knew if I turned left, the four of us would die instantly. If I turned right, we might have a chance. So I swerved right, and I don't know how, but we landed between a telephone pole and a road sign and narrowly escaped a collision with the racing cars.

For many months after the near-accident I was baffled. Over and over again I went to the scene and reenacted what happened from the point I had seen the cars coming. How had I known I was in danger? How had my car gotten to the side of the road without a collision? And then there was the most baffling question: How had I seen the cars coming in enough time to save us? It actually wasn't possible, because the cars had been coming around a double curve. If I hadn't had an advance warning, we would have collided, head-on, with both of them.

I feel God saved me that day. It was his way of saying, "I need you back and I want you to have faith that I will always be with you."

"Don't jump!"

TRISH BARFIELD,
Retired Real Estate Business Owner

I rarely paid my train fare when I was young, preferring to spend my hard-earned wages on candy and treats. One Sunday I was on the second train ride of a trip to the beach to see my boyfriend. I saw the ticket collector approaching the carriage I was in. Alarmed, I went to jump out of the opposite side of the train from the station—something I had done before.

Apart from myself, the carriage was empty. As I prepared to jump, just as the train halted, I heard a loud male voice say, "Don't jump!" I turned around, expecting to see the ticket inspector, but there was no one there. At the same instant, a freight train came whooshing by. Had I jumped, I would have gone into the path of that train.

I know the hand of God touched my life at that moment. I am not religious. I regard "God" as part of everyday life. I don't have to pray or be religious to see that side of life. It seems I was not meant to die that day, and I will never forget this warning.

"God made me cunning"

SHIRLEY BLAKE, *Teacher*

I was fifty-nine years old and living by myself. I was tutoring two young underprivileged boys when a man came to my door asking for them. The boys saw him and immediately ran, leaving the house through the back door.

I had no idea why they were so afraid until I turned back around and the man punched me. I yelled out, "God help me!" and he hit me again. Every time I screamed for God, the man punched me. He then proceeded to rape me. I screamed out for God's help as he penetrated my body. I felt Satan's presence engulfing me. And then, all of a sudden, I felt the comforting presence of God and I heard him tell me to be still. I knew God wouldn't give me anything I couldn't handle, and a sense of calm washed over me.

For several hours I was raped repeatedly and violently. And then the man forced me to make him dinner. After dinner, he took me to my bedroom and began raping me again, with acts that were unspeakable. Seven hours passed. Despite the horror around me, I still had the beautiful presence of God there with me the whole time. I was at peace. And then God made me cunning. I had to be. I said to the man, "So, will I see you tomorrow?" He hesitated briefly, questioning what I had said. And then he spoke: "Okay, I'll wait for you in the backyard." The rape stopped. He got dressed, threatened to kill me if I left the house, and then walked out the door. I immediately ran to a friend, who took me to the hospital.

A policewoman came to me in my hospital room and I told her I would press charges. I described the man as having a severe burn mark on his chest. The police immediately knew who he was. He had been raping and beating women since he was twelve years old, but because he had always threatened to kill them if they told, no one had ever pressed charges against him. He had been terrorizing an entire community for years.

The next day, a young boy I knew came to my bedside and told me a man had raped him, but he had never told anyone. After he left, women and young girls came to me as I recuperated, all telling me they had been raped and asking me how I was able to face it. I told them God's spirit had helped me.

My perpetrator received a ten-year prison sentence. I am grateful my experience prevented him from hurting others.

"Why me?"

DIANNE MOORE, *Retired Accountant*

Although I was a member of the Salvation Army, I was still seeking a real belief in God when on September 20, 1982, I was told by doctors that I had retinal dystrophy and would probably be blind within twelve months. I was devastated. I even contemplated suicide.

A few days after my diagnosis, I was vacuuming the house and I really took God to task. "Why me?" I asked. "Why give me a better-than-average IQ when the loss of my sight will make all that useless?" At that moment, a voice said, "You twit! That very intelligence will help you cope!" Those were the exact words I heard. I couldn't believe it. I looked around, but I was alone.

At that moment I lost all the anger and resentment I had been feeling. I simply settled down, tried not to worry about my eyes, and just got on with my life.

That was twenty-four years ago, and recently I passed the eye exam for my driver's license without the use of glasses! Yes, I still have retinal dystrophy—or macular degeneration, as it is now called—but it is moving so slowly that I shall probably go before my sight does! I might just have committed suicide in 1982 if that voice had not given me the courage to deal with the future, whatever it might be.

"Who do you think you are?"

MANDY JONES,
Passenger Information Officer, Public Transport Authority

My nana had been sick for many years with dementia, and with each passing year it got worse. I couldn't see the point in her having to live like this for so many years when there was no quality of life.

One day I was sitting outside and was in deep concentration for a long period of time, more than half an hour. I was wishing that Nan could die and be put out of what I perceived to be her misery.

Eventually I got up and went into my home. I had taken two steps through the door when a loud, deep, strong, booming voice said, "Who do you think you are that you should decide when someone should live or die?"

I stopped in my tracks and then I looked around—not really expecting to see anything, but not knowing what else to do. No one was with me, and I realized it was God and that he had told me off. I walked around the house very quietly for the rest of the day!

This is the only time I've heard his voice, and it left a very big impression on me.

"No!"

MICHELLE ROBINSON, *Hair Salon Owner*

I was going through a particularly rough time in my life. I had just broken up with my boyfriend of six years and had moved into an apartment of my own. I was having difficulty making decisions and was very sad and confused. Then one night my ex-boyfriend showed up at my new apartment. He said we had both made a mistake and hadn't tried hard enough to work it out. He pleaded with me to get back together with him.

After he left, I walked outside. I honestly didn't know what to do. I just didn't feel I could make another decision in my life. I cried out in desperation, "Help me. I don't know what to do! Am I supposed to go back to him?" Immediately, and seemingly out of nowhere, came a loud, clear, commanding voice: "No!"

I looked around, even though I instinctively knew the voice hadn't come from a person.

I'll never forget it. No one was with me or near me, and the answer couldn't have been louder. It was guidance, and I felt comforted by it. I can't explain why. It was a bit frightening, but at the same time, I knew immediately who it was. I now know I don't have to ask for guidance, because I'm always getting it.

"Move over!"

LEA MULQUEEN, *Photographer/Pet Sitter*

I had just driven my daughter to her class at the University of Baltimore, and I was returning home at about 10 a.m., on Interstate 83. The traffic was light and I had the far left lane all to myself. All of a sudden I heard a voice say, "Move over!" I remember looking over at the empty passenger seat and seeing nothing. A few seconds later, I heard it again: "Move over!" This time I remember saying, "Why should I?" Immediately the voice yelled, "Move over *now!*" This time I didn't hesitate and switched lanes. A couple of seconds later, a car came barreling at me head-on in the far left lane on my side of the divided highway.

The voice kept me from colliding at sixty miles an hour with another car. That car was being followed by police. I learned later that they were chasing a man in a stolen car who had entered the highway via the exit ramp.

"Who am I?"

KAREN SCHMA,
Sales Representative, Textile Leasing Company

In 1985 I reached a crossroad in my life. I had a nervous breakdown and quit my job, where I was earning a great income and had security. I quit because I could no longer live with myself. I was having sexual relations with my married boss to get along with him and to keep my job working for one of the world's largest automobile makers. I moved back home with my parents and fell apart emotionally after realizing I had sacrificed all the morals I had been raised with.

It was at this time that I learned I needed surgery for ovarian cysts. After the surgery, my gynecologist asked me into his office. "Do you know who I am?" he asked. "You're my doctor," I replied matter-of-factly. But all of a sudden it was as if time had stopped, and everything froze as a loud, powerful voice came from him saying, "Who am I?" And then repeated, "Who am I?" It was a deep male voice and seemed as if it were being channeled through him.

I knew, after all I had been through, that it was the Higher Force. "God!" I replied. "You are my Father, God." Immediately a bright white light encircled me. I listened as the man recapped my sins. I felt terrible and ashamed. And then he said things that made me feel better. He told me I was a good person and that I brought happiness to other people. He told me that one day I would be rewarded. He reminded me that I was surrounded by love from my parents and family, and that it would all work out. He then said that the last part of my life would be the easiest.

I've never told anyone this story before because I didn't think anyone would believe me. But it did happen. After this very strange experience, I felt total love and wasn't afraid of anything. I now know that there is a God and that he is watching me.

"Get back in the car!"

MELINDA KOPP, *Teacher*

I t was 1984. I was eighteen years old and a college freshman. I was enrolled in summer school and was traveling the Natchez Trace Parkway to and from my night classes. It was not a heavily traveled road at that time, and, of course, this was long before the time of cell phones.

One night we had a test and the teacher let us leave an hour early. No one was expecting me home yet, and I looked forward to surprising my family by eating supper with them that night. It was around eight o'clock. The sun had set and it was getting dark. About twelve miles from home, I got a flat. I opened my trunk to find that the spare had the wrong rim and that the lugs on the wheel did not match the lugs on the spare. There was no jack.

I was near a crossroad and a relative of mine lived about two miles away, so I got out of the car and started for the inter-section, walking downhill in the twilight. Suddenly a man's voice said, "Melinda, get back in the car. *Now!*" I stopped and looked around to see who was talking to me but there wasn't anybody there. I thought, "Is this God talking to me?" So I said, "Lord? Is that you?" Again the voice said, "Get back in the car!" At this point there wasn't any doubt in my mind that it was God speaking and I realized that something was about to happen. I didn't argue. I got right back into the car.

All of a sudden it was very dark and I was getting nervous.

I sat in the car and said, "Okay, what now?" Just then I saw lights approaching. But something compelled me to sit still. The car passed. A few minutes later, another car approached. Now the voice said, "Flash your lights." I did, and the car stopped. It was a family friend.

I truly believe that the voice I heard was God's. He provided a rescue for me that night. Who knows what might have happened if I had struck out walking or had signaled that first car.

Today my relationship with God is extremely personal. I am a minister of music and youth at my church. I believe I had this work to do and was preserved through the grace of God.

"Get out of the car!"

ARMANDO DEANGELIS, *Retired Federal Agent*

It was late in the afternoon of December 3, 1967. I was riding in a car with two of my friends, Robert Signorelli (whom we called Siggy) and Billy Ward. Siggy and I were from Medford, Massachusetts, and Billy was from the next city over, Somerville. We were all young men at the time, only twenty.

As we were approaching the corner at Harvard and Main, where we hung out in Medford, I heard the voice of God calling to me. It was an actual voice. He was saying, "Butch [my nickname], get out of the car. Get out of the car!" Billy was driving, and I asked him to let me out at the corner. They dropped me off and drove away.

At eleven o'clock that night, I got a call at home from my best friend, Tony, who told me that Siggy and Billy had been in a car accident on Medford Street in Somerville. Siggy died that night, and Billy passed away the following day.

That moment made me get down on my hands and knees and say, "Thank you for saving me." The experience strengthened my belief in God.

"Go back and help that man!"

MIKE HILTON, *Importer/Distributor*

A few years ago, I had to take some sample air-conditioning equipment from the city I live in to demonstrate it in a smaller city three hours north. I didn't have a trailer at the time, so I borrowed an old one from Pastor Stan, a minister at the church I attend.

The trailer was fully loaded and off I went. But an hour into the trip, at a point where the highway stretched out for miles and miles with no houses, the trailer blew a tire. I managed to stop the car without rolling the trailer. I then unloaded the trunk to get my jack and lug wrench, only to discover that the wheels on my car were a size larger than the old trailer's. The lug wrench would not fit the nuts on the trailer.

Somehow I managed to get every one of the nuts off except one—which, for some reason, was a size smaller. No matter how I tried, there was no way I could undo this last nut. Cars passed, and no one stopped.

A station wagon sped past me, and I thought of Pastor Stan. He had taught me that when I pray, I should pray out loud. So I stood up, lifted my hands in the air, and said aloud, "Lord, I'm in trouble and I need your help."

Within minutes, a station wagon pulled up. A young man got out and said, "Wow, you look as though you are in trouble." I explained my predicament, and his response was "No worries. I think I can help." He reached into the back of his wagon and pulled out a socket set, and we found a socket that fit the remaining nut.

We took off the wheel and the man asked what I was going to do next. I told him that I would have to unhook the trailer and take the flat tire back to the nearest town. "How are you going to do the nuts up?" he asked. I told him I'd purchase a new lug wrench while having the puncture mended. He asked if I was going back to the city, and I told him I was. So he said, "Don't buy a new lug wrench. Here's my address. Drop the sockets off at my home on your way back."

I thanked him profusely as he walked away. Before he got into his car, he turned to me and said, "You know a funny thing happened to me as I was driving past you. I heard a voice say to me, 'Stop! Go back and help that man!'"

I figure the moment he heard that voice was about the same time I prayed out loud, "Lord, I'm in trouble and I need your help."

"It's all good news"

LINDSAY NEWLAND BOWKER,
Vacation Rental Owner

On my mother's last day, there was a brief pause at noon in the chain of well-wishers who had gathered to be a presence and comfort for her in her final hours. She was very tired and had turned away the unappetizing tray of hospital food. She was glad I had brought her some slices of orange flesh ("orange supreme"), thinking they would be refreshing and easy to eat. As she took her first bite, she said, "This is very weird. I'm already dead, but I can taste this orange—not like regular tasting, not like before. I know I'm physically here with you—that we can touch each other, hear each other—but it's not as before. It's weird. I'm already dead."

I didn't know what to say or what she meant. I didn't reply. When she finished as much as she could eat of her orange, she said, "So, what do you know about this? What does it mean? I know I'm dead and yet I'm here. How is that possible?" Again, I wasn't sure what to say and didn't want to question her.

She rested a while and then stirred. We were alone. I smiled. She smiled back—radiant and beautiful, unafraid and full of grace. I said, "Mom, remember, when I don't see you, I expect to see you here—on my shoulder. Remember, you promised to come back as my guardian angel." "Oh," she said, "I forgot to tell you. They said I can't do that. They said you already have someone with you who has always been there. They said I will know about you somehow, be aware when you are happy or sad, have news of you. But they have another job for me, and I must do what I am asked." Again, I said nothing, and she said nothing more about it.

My sister returned with her family, and the room was full again. My mom spoke to each person with such wisdom and grace. After a while my sister and I both put our heads to Mom and kissed her at the same time. She said, "I'm sorry I died today." We both answered by saying, "We will miss you so much and love you so much."

My mom quickly fell into a sleep from which she would never awaken.

As I was preparing her eulogy that week, I kept getting stuck. I wanted to say the right thing to bring healing to my sister and her children. I thought about what Mom had said about already being dead. I begged God, Mom, anyone who would listen, to tell me whether Mom was already dead as we watched her body gasp and struggle for breath in her final moments, or whether she suffered and felt what we saw. That night a loud voice, not my mom's, woke me from sleep. It was like a telepathic voice, inside me, not in the room, and it said, "In time all your questions will be answered. But don't worry, it's all good news."

This experience simplified my faith. It strengthened my certainty that there is life after death and that there is a Divine, benevolent spirit that binds, guides, protects, and nurtures all living things. I believe life is about phases and different states of being, of which life on earth is only one. Now when the gospel is about Lazarus or Christ rising from the dead and appearing to his disciples after death, there is no mystery of faith. I know it happens to ordinary people everywhere, every day. It happened to my mom. I witnessed it. She was dead, yet present in her body. I also know now that God listens and gives us the answers we need to clear the clutter from our spirit.

"Will you have her?"

TOM DORNAN, *Pastor*

Twenty years ago I was falling through the end of a very hard fifteen-year marriage. I had four children and was feeling desperate about the unhappiness that had come upon us. Counseling was not working and prayers seemed to go unanswered. In an effort to gain some peace, I moved in with my mother and started the annulment process with the Roman Catholic Church and the divorce process with lawyers.

During this time I could find no hope for the situation at hand. I was praying that the Lord would take me through death, rather than make me live a life of shame. No one in my own family had ever divorced. The everyday demands of being a father, worker, and son began to take their toll on me. I needed *out* of relationships and life. I needed some rest!

The rest that came was unexpected. I was asked and decided to join several business colleagues for a conference being held in the Midwest (I lived in Boston). It was good to go to workshops during the day and quietly rest during the night. I thought, "Perhaps a single life of celibacy will bring me the least pain." Then God made his plan known to me during a game of volleyball.

On the fourth day of the six-day conference, the volleyball net was set up. I was not prone to play volleyball as a usual part of my life because I was too busy. But I was resting from being busy and decided to play. As the line shifted during the course of play, I found myself front and center at the net. Directly in front of me was a younger woman. That's when the God moment happened. A voice from deep within me that I can only describe as God's voice said, "This person in front of you will be the love of your life for the rest of your life. Will you have her?" As I looked at her, I heard my soul respond, "Yes, Lord, but how will this be?" The response was "I will provide all—just trust in me!"

During the whole time of the "God conversation," I never moved, and neither did the woman in front of me. I felt that the line had shifted around us, but I had no sense of time. Immediately after the "voice" left me, the game was suddenly over. I moved to the side of the net and met the young woman who had just been "divinely" introduced to me. Her name was Dawn. She was younger, single, never married, and a Protestant. I was a failed Catholic, divorcing, with four children. I flew home two days later after exchanging contact information with her.

Over the following six months I made no contact and received no inquiry from her. Then it was Christmastime, and a letter arrived that brought some resolution to my own question, "God, what was that volleyball-net conversation about anyway?" The young woman wrote about her family, schooling, and hopes for life. I was happy to receive her letter: it was brightness during some very dark times.

As we began to correspond, we made plans to attend another conference being held in the springtime. It was during the spring conference that I instinctively knew God wanted to provide for my happiness through a marriage to Dawn.

Five months later, I was sleeping when the same voice came to me again and said only two words: "Go now!" I went into work that day and gave two weeks' notice. I had no job to go to and had never lived in the Midwest. I asked the children if they would come with me, but they said no, preferring to stay with their mother and friends.

And so I took off for the Midwest from New England. As I

drove into the outskirts of Chicago, I called my mother to check in. She said a man had called and left a message. It was a former work acquaintance. He had heard that I was moving to the Midwest and wanted me to contact a person in Chicago for a possible job. I called the number and was told I could be interviewed right away at a hotel near O'Hare Airport. I went to the interview wearing only my traveling clothes—jeans and a T-shirt—and I got the job. The job turned out to be in St. Paul, Minnesota, thirty-five miles from where Dawn lived!

The rest of the story is now part of a seventeen-year marriage that has been blessed with two children. Dawn has been a wonderful stepmother to my other four children. And although she never heard the "voice" I heard, she never moved from her place in front of that volleyball net that day eighteen years ago. God has surely been true to his word: she is the love of my life. With her I have found rest, true love, and peace. And for this gift, I am most thankful to God.

"I felt a surge of energy from head to toe"

DENISE ROLLAND,
Retired Executive Search Consulting Firm Owner

From my early childhood I always questioned the existence of God. Coming from a violent and abusive family, I learned to trust no one but myself. I was an atheist. God had never been there for me.

I worked hard to build a good life. I did several years of therapy and went back to school to earn a degree in psychology from McGill University so that I could take care of my sisters. But something was missing.

In 1993, after having resigned from my job as vice president of a large international search firm, I came home feeling very depressed and full of doubts. Even though my decision was well planned and thought-out, I was immersed in feelings of discouragement and vulnerability. I had decided to start my own firm, and with this decision had come all the feelings of financial insecurity and fear that such an adventure entails.

At around eleven o'clock the next morning, I was sitting in the living room of my country home—emotionally drained and depressed. Suddenly I felt a surge of energy from head to toe. My body was filled with unconditional love. At the same time, I heard a voice say, "I will always be here for you. Don't be scared."

What an experience! I will never forget it. I now know that I'm privileged to have experienced God and his vast love and kindness.

"It was a voice—not a thought"

JANICE OLSZANSKI STOVKA,
Retired Greeting Card Merchandiser/Grandmother

I was at the lowest point in my life. My mother was very ill. The thought of her approaching death made me inconsolable. For fifty years she had been my loving mom, my rock, my friend. I had lived next door to her my whole adult life. I couldn't imagine never seeing her sitting in her favorite chair or talking to Dad again. The thought was too much for me to bear.

For six months I prayed to the Holy Spirit for consolation. I asked God to give me strength for the coming trials my family—especially my father—would have to go through.

And then late one night as I was crying and filled with sadness, I heard a voice in my mind. It was a voice—not a thought. It was soft and gentle and said very clearly, "It will be okay. She will be okay." And then slowly a powerful sense of peace came over me. It was an amazing moment. God spoke to me and answered my prayers. I have no doubt.

When the time came for my mother to pass out of this life and into the next, I can truly say I was at peace. I prayed for the knowledge that my mom would be okay, and she is, I'm sure of it, because God told me so.

"IS THERE ANY WAY YOU CAN HELP ME?"

Having a Prayer Answered

"As I was getting high, my body shut down"

JOSÉ ROJAS, *Job Developer for Welfare Recipients*

I know God exists. I had served as an altar boy when the mass was in Latin. I was a believer. My parents instilled the fear of God in me through the Catholic Church. However, I drifted away from the principles I had been taught by a very caring and loving mother. When I became a young adult, I started looking for excitement and instant gratification and started using drugs, especially crack cocaine.

I was addicted to the stuff for twenty-two years, and although I wanted to stop using, it was impossible for me. There was no way out and, believe me, I tried to get clean with all the energy I could muster—to no avail.

For the last three years of this addiction I was living in an abandoned building (with no utilities) and eating out of trash cans. I knew God would someday come to my rescue someway, somehow—I just didn't know when.

One day, after I had been up for about five days and nights, I came home to the abandoned building and, as I was getting high, my body shut down. I woke up two days later at about one o'clock in the morning. When I went to leave the room I was in, I saw a half-broken full-length mirror on the door—something I had never seen before.

I went to take hold of the doorknob, and when I did, I saw the reflection of my hand in the mirror. I was not afraid but was wondering what was happening and how this mirror got there.

Curiosity set in, and I undressed and returned to stand in front of the mirror. I was able to see myself completely, in a worn-out body, very thin and ragged, and I could smell the stench of not taking care of my personal hygiene for months.

I put on the ragged clothes again, and when I was leaving through the same door, the mirror was gone. God showed me that there remained a flicker of light in me and that he was there to help me change—if I wanted to! As I walked out the door, I said the following prayer: "God, I know that what is impossible for me is possible for you. Show me what you can do with this imitation of a man."

That happened on New Year's Day, 1993. From that moment on, God has brought me along to be involved in his business every day. I now see everything in my life from a different perspective. It's as if a fog has lifted. And every time I reach for the handle on a door, I relive that moment when God touched me.

"I sank beneath the water"

KENNETH MORTIMER, *Management Consultant*

My wife and I were living in Christchurch, New Zealand, when her sister Sarah came for a visit. My wife worked the night shift as a nurse and slept during the day on Saturdays. So on this particular Saturday I decided to take Sarah and my two children to the beach in a rubber inflatable raft.

We entered the raft and paddled toward the beach. But the tide was stronger than I had anticipated and, even with all our paddling, we weren't making any progress. I decided to jump into the water, grab the rope, and swim everyone into shore. I wasn't successful. I wasn't a strong swimmer and I just wasn't making any headway against the current.

I decided to swim in, get the car, and meet the boat wherever it landed. I headed toward land, but the current was too strong and I was swept away. I veered toward some moored yachts and grabbed for an anchor cable, but I couldn't get it. As my children watched, I started to go down.

I sank beneath the water three times and then, in desperation, screamed out to God. "Jesus, Mary, Joseph, save me! This would be a waste!" The next second, an arm grabbed me.

Three lifeguards had heard Sarah's screams for help and saved my life.

Skeptics will say it was my sister-in-law's screams for help that saved my life. I say, "Say what you like. I know what I know. As soon as I said that prayer, I was saved."

"What if?"

DONALD MACHOVOE, *Mechanical Engineer*

After five years of marriage my wife and I were faced with the hardship of having no work and no place to live. I had heard of some job openings in North Carolina and contacted a company I was told was hiring. They said they would get back to me. However, we decided the prospects looked good and that we would drive there with our three children (ages four and three years, and a one-month old) and all of our worldly possessions in a U-Haul trailer. I had received two unemployment checks, and that was all the money we had to travel from western New York to North Carolina.

As it turned out, the place we went to was not hiring at that time, and we were told to go home. They would call us if they decided to hire me. So, with just enough money to fill the car with gas, we started the sixteen-hour drive back to New York.

At lunchtime the children were crying that they were hungry. We found enough change to buy a McDonald's burger and fries, which satisfied their hunger for the time being. Later that evening, sometime after ten o'clock, we had made our way to Williamsport, Pennsylvania, and the children were crying that they were hungry again and I was very low on gas. Not knowing what to do, I saw a closed gas station and pulled in to look at the map to see just how far we needed to go to get back to my parents' home. It was at this time that I spotted a soda machine in

the shadows and told my wife that I could break into it and perhaps get enough money for gas and food. She was against it but
agreed that we needed to do something.

I took the tire iron out of the trunk and started toward the
machine, but something told me not to do it and to get back to
the car. I returned and put the tire iron into the trunk, and just
then a police cruiser pulled up and asked if everything was all
right. We told him we thought we had a flat and I was just
checking the tires. He followed us out of the lot. I looked at my
wife. We both knew that if I had not turned back, I would have
been caught in the act.

As we started driving up a mountain, I told my wife that we
needed gas and only had enough for another fifty miles, if we
were lucky. Being religious, she began to pray. She prayed for
God to help us. When she finished, she said she had a feeling
everything would be okay.

Twenty minutes after my wife prayed for help, I spotted a
roadside multiplex with gas, food, and a motel and decided to
stop and ask if they would trust me for some gas to fill up the car.
The manager said he wasn't accustomed to giving out gas, but
because it was cold and snowing (and the kids were crying), he
agreed.

After filling up the tank, he noticed that the tire on the
trailer was flat. So we called the number for U-Haul and the
lady on the phone said there was no way they could fix the tire
that late at night. She suggested I stay there until a truck could
come out to repair the tire in the morning. I told her that I had
no money and could not pay for a room or food. So she asked if
she could talk to the manager. She told him to give us a room
for the night along with dinner and breakfast and to bill U-Haul
for it.

We left the next day believing we had just witnessed a miracle,
as there was no other way to explain what had happened to us.

I sometimes think back to that day and wonder, "What if?" What if I had been caught breaking into the soda machine and arrested? With an arrest, I would not have been able to get security clearances to work. And worse, our children may well have been taken from us. Yes, what if?

"Lord, give me strength"

LARRY MERRILL, *Lawyer*

I was participating in a kayak race. The weather was awful. It was windy with pouring rain. I had two miles to go. No one else was near me, either ahead or behind. Although I anticipated no problem finishing, I was becoming weary. As I came around a corner where I knew the wind would be right in my face for about half a mile, I casually said, "Lord, give me strength."

I thought back to a race I'd been in a few years before. The wind was blowing powerfully against me. At a spot where the river narrowed and the current increased, I went past a rocky ledge twice and was blown back past it each time. I was getting close to desperate. I prayed that the wind would diminish, but my prayer wasn't answered. In the end, though, I found the strength to finish.

This time, when I said, "Lord, give me strength," I got an immediate answer. The wind doubled! I just burst out laughing. I had asked for strength and I was getting the workout that would give it to me. I laughed for half a mile, which took about twice as long as it should have. When I turned the corner and got out of the wind, I looked up and said, "You enjoyed that, didn't you?" I could almost hear him say, "Yes, and so did you!" And I did! It was nice to know he was listening and has a sense of humor.

"This was my answer"

ROBERT MCALISTER, *Pastor*

Upon returning from ten years as a missionary in the city of Kiev, in Ukraine, I decided to spend several days at a monastery outside of Charleston, South Carolina, to pray and seek the Lord. While I was there, I kept asking God to speak to my heart, to tell me what he wanted me to hear. After three days, I didn't feel I was hearing anything—until the last morning.

As I sat at the little desk in my small room asking the same question, my cell phone rang. It was a lady from the church where I serve as pastor in Lexington, South Carolina. She didn't know where I was or what I was doing. She told me that she had been praying that morning and in her heart she felt she should call me and tell me that God loved me and saw me as his child. She said he was pleased with me and that I should keep going and not be discouraged.

I am not one who looks for the miraculous to be convinced, but I am convinced this was my answer and that God spoke to me through this lady. I hung up the phone and, all alone in my room, I smiled and knew that my God was real. Coincidence, some may say? I don't believe that for a moment.

"Is there any way you can help me?"

RICK FEHR, *Window Washer*

I didn't grow up in the church. I did believe in something, but I wasn't sure it was God.

In 1996 I found out I had T-cell non-Hodgkin lymphoma and was given a 4 to 10 percent chance of survival. I don't know why, but I asked, "God, if you're there, is there any way you can help me?" I told him I would change my ways, which meant no more drinking, smoking, or running around with different women.

After nearly a year of treatment, I was in remission and had forgotten about what I had said to God.

Three years later, in 1999, my cancer came back. This time I made it my mission to take God into my life and change for the better. The act changed my life forever.

Within months I met and married my wife. And then, despite my having been told I could never father children, she became pregnant. Nine months later, my son—my hero—was born.

Again I am cancer-free and love God more than anything. In everything I do, I put my trust in God's hands.

"I had begun to worry I would never get married"

RAY EDWARDS, *Home Sales Consultant*

I was a bachelor at twenty-nine and had been invited to a wedding. It was an Episcopal wedding, so there were ample opportunities to pray. At this stage of my life I had begun to worry I would never find my soul mate and get married. As I sat in the church listening to my friends say their vows, there was another prompt to pray. I prayed that God would finally show me the woman I would spend my life with. I then felt a calm come over me and heard, in my mind, that it would happen soon. I didn't give it any more thought that day, assuming it had been my subconscious reassuring me.

Two weeks later to the day, I was invited to a Super Bowl party at a nearby apartment complex. I'm not a sports person at all, so I originally declined to go. But something compelled me to go anyway.

I went to the party and sat on the floor, talking to various strangers and half-watching the game on TV. I noticed that a chair nearby was unoccupied, so I went to it and sat down. A couple of minutes later a very intriguing woman informed me that I had taken her chair and would I please move!

That was seventeen years ago, and we are still very happily married with a thirteen-year-old son.

I had never experienced the direct power of prayer up to that point. I have since then and know the Lord does hear our prayers and answers in his own way.

"I found it very difficult to trust"

JANE STILL, *Journalist*

I was a single parent at the age of twenty-one with two tiny children and very little family or friendly support after my husband walked out. I had a number of faith experiences over the next few years, though, that sustained me. The one that stands out the most happened just after I met my current husband.

With abuse issues in my past, I found it very difficult to trust, and with one failed marriage, I was finding it hard to believe that my current boyfriend, David, loved me or would really want to take our relationship to a deep level. David had gone away on holiday, and I spent one very dark night on the sofa sobbing to God that I knew it would all go wrong, as everything in my life always did. I was doomed to be left alone as punishment for my failed marriage.

After sobbing, I felt a tremendous peace and then prayed, "I'll give it over to your hands, Lord." As soon as I prayed those words, the phone rang. It was David saying he missed me too much and was cutting his holiday short to be with me.

We were married a year later and now have five beautiful daughters.

"I let out all the heartache and loneliness"

MAGGIE GEENE, *Graduate Student*

I was a thirty-five-year-old wife and mother of four. I had never doubted the existence of God, but for a few years I felt I had no connection to God at all. In my faith we call a time like this the dark night of the soul.

I felt alone. I was in deep despair and received no joy or consolation from the practice of my faith as I had before. Every time I prayed, it seemed dry and artificial. Even though I still went through the motions of prayer and went to church every Sunday, God wasn't listening or, worse, just didn't care about me.

One weekend my son and I were attending a Mom-and-Me Cub Scout campout. Before dawn one morning I found myself wide awake. I got up and walked down to the lake. It was still dark, but I could see a mist rolling over the water as the sun started to rise.

I sat on a picnic table and meditated on how alone I felt. It suddenly occurred to me that maybe this was how Jesus felt on the cross when he cried out, "My God, my God, why have you abandoned me?" I began to pray and pour my heart out to God. I let out all the heartache and loneliness I felt as if I were talking to someone sitting next to me on the picnic table.

As I did this, I became aware of a deep sense of peace flooding through me. The sensation shook me to my core. Sitting there, I began to cry, but they were tears of joy.

As the morning sun broke over the lake and the mist burned away, my dark night lifted. I could feel God's presence again. I realized that I could converse with him the same way I did with someone I loved. I called out, and in my anguish he answered my cry.

"I prayed for a fair wind and a miracle"

ALAN BOND, *Entrepreneur*

It was 1983. I was heading up Australia's yachting challenge for the America's Cup trophy. America had held the cup for 132 years in the longest winning streak in the history of sport.

After four challenges spanning fifteen years, we believed we had the fastest boat and the best crew, but we were still completely in the hands of the elements. We were in the seventh and last race of the America's Cup. Coming up to the sixth leg of the course in Newport, Rhode Island, we were hopelessly behind Dennis Conner's *Liberty*. It was so bad that many Australians watching the race on television started turning off their sets. There was no hope of overtaking *Liberty* on the second-to-last leg, with only two parts of the race left to complete.

It now looked as though even with the fastest boat, the best sails, and the best crew, we were once again going to fail. I had a headache and went below in my tender, the observation boat. The boat was connected to the instruments on the *Australia II* yacht so I could pick up the speed, wind directions, and performance of the yacht against a computerized theoretical model. Knowing the relative speed of the boat and the wind conditions, I realized that a loss was inevitable and that once again America would hold the America's Cup.

Right then and there—at that very moment—I prayed. And there were many people throughout Australia praying at the same time, I'm sure. I prayed that there would be a fair wind and that a miracle would happen.

As we came around the top mark, Dennis Conner was half a mile ahead and there was hardly any wind. The boys put up the small spinnaker on *Australia II,* and in the next ten minutes a miracle occurred. A wind came up behind our yacht. I remember that my headache disappeared and I felt the tension fade away. The crew called down from the top deck of the tender, saying, "Alan, come up immediately! Something's happening. *Australia II* is catching *Liberty!*" The wind had come up behind our yacht, not Dennis's yacht, and pushed *Australia II,* in the length of 2.5 miles, into the lead.

We overtook Dennis Conner at the bottom mark. But it wasn't over yet. An almighty battle occurred, and it took forty-eight tacks to get us to the finish line. In the end, *Australia II* managed to finish some thirty-eight seconds ahead of *Liberty.*

But that's not the end of the story. The next morning there was a photo shoot. We put up our sails and made one tack with the yacht. With that tack, the headboard of the mainsail broke and the mainsail fell down. I felt this was the end of the message I had received from God the day before. Not only had a miracle been performed in winning the race, but the boat had held together to get us across the finish line. From this experience I learned that prayers are answered.

"I was petrified to go back into the house"

SHARON KELLY, *Housewife*

One night in 2001 while in my house, I felt I was being touched by something I couldn't see. It scared the life out of me. I knew there was a presence in the house.

The next morning I packed up the kids for school and left with them. I couldn't go back home. At the school I told another mother what had happened and she gave me the phone number of a medium. I called the medium from the school and told her what had happened to me the night before. She said she was booked up with appointments for the next two days and couldn't see me until after that. But I was petrified to go back into the house. I became very upset and asked God over and over again to please help me because I didn't want to go back.

A few hours later I realized I had to go back to the house to get some things for my baby. I was so frightened that I was crying as I packed the stuff into a bag. The phone rang. It was the medium. She said, "Do you know God loves you very much? I have to come to your house tonight because every one of my appointments for the next two days has canceled." Her words made me cry because I knew straightaway that God had heard my plea.

That night friends took the children while the medium performed a ritual to cleanse the house. At one point during the cleansing, the room we were in lit up brightly, and I said, "What was that?" The medium said, "You don't know? That was the light of God." Four hours later, when she finished, I felt as if a weight had been lifted from me. It was amazing. The presence, who I was told was a young girl who had died in the house, disappeared.

I've always believed in God. This experience reaffirmed my belief.

"The darkness was forced back!"

ANITA STAADEN, *Veterinary Ophthalmologist*

I was nine years old when my family started going to a church retreat at Easter time. It was a wonderful experience. We stayed in cabins and shared meals and fellowship with other families.

I had been going for eleven years when, after many years of happy and uplifting experiences, everything went wrong. At this camp there was a feeling of disease. Instead of people feeling happy and relaxed, they were uncomfortable and tense. The fun wasn't there; the warmth of fellowship wasn't there. On the last night of camp, my cousin came to me and said, "I don't know why, but I feel really terrible. I'm not enjoying camp this year. I just want to go home." And then she started to cry.

I knew just how she felt because I was feeling the same way. I hadn't realized others were feeling it too. For a while we held each other and wept. Then we decided to do something about it. We decided to go down to the chapel and pray. It was rare for me to pray with someone, and probably for her, too, but we both felt it was the only way to remedy the situation.

I will never forget the feeling of darkness in that chapel as we prayed. It was worse than a dark night. The darkness was thick, as though the air was black smoke, and it was humming and pulsating. It was trying to close in on us. It would move in around us and then fall back a little, press in, move out, but each time edging closer toward us. We were surrounded by palpable evil, evil that knew we were trying to get rid of it. It was trying to intimidate us, to defeat us. We were filled with negative feelings—sadness, disappointment, discomfort, depression.

As we prayed, the most remarkable thing happened. The darkness was forced back! It was still pulsating and pressing, but it was being forced back. The power of our prayers was forcing it back! We kept on praying, and all of a sudden the darkness was gone, almost with a pop. Just like that, it disappeared and with it went our feelings of depression. We felt relief and joy and victory. But most of all we felt surprise that the power of our prayer had not only repelled this unnatural darkness but actually caused it to vanish.

We walked back to camp joyful and relieved, and from that moment on, the mood in the camp changed. That night there was a very powerful and uplifting worship followed by lots of sharing, warmth, and bonding among the campers. What had looked as if it would be the worst camp ever turned out to be the best. I left that camp on a high like I had never experienced before. For me, that very real experience shared with my cousin is my best evidence that God exists and that real evil exists, not only in people's behavior but as an entity all of its own. It taught me the power of prayer.

"She thought the baby was dead"

SHAWN MILLER, *Certified Public Accountant*

My wife was thirty-five weeks pregnant. The pregnancy hadn't been easy for her. She had gestational diabetes, too much amniotic fluid, and a heart condition. She woke up one morning and told me she thought the baby was dead. I stood there in shock. She said she hadn't felt the baby move since midnight and it was now eight in the morning. We called the doctor and were told to go directly to the hospital.

At the hospital, a nurse put a device on my wife's belly to monitor the baby's heart rate. Good news: the nurse found a heartbeat. The next thing she had to check for was movement. She did this by checking the fluctuation in the baby's heart rate. Every time the baby moves, his heart rate changes. The bad news was that the baby's heart rate was not fluctuating. The machine generated a relatively flat line that showed no movement.

While my wife was connected to the machine, I began reading a book about miracles. The writings in this book spoke of faith and the results of faith. I read that in John 14:12–14, Jesus said: "I tell you the truth, anyone who has faith in me will do what I have been doing. He will do even greater things than these, because I am going to the Father. And I will do whatever you ask in my name, so that the Son may bring glory to the Father. You may ask me for anything in my name, and I will do it." I immediately wrote this verse in my journal and asked God to help us through this difficult time.

The ultrasound was next. The test found that there was no breathing and no movement of the baby's arms or legs. My heart dropped. We watched the ultrasound technician monitor the baby for thirty minutes without any sign of life except the heartbeat. We asked her if the baby was all right and she told us we'd have to talk to the doctor.

After the test, my wife sat in a wheelchair in the hallway and we prayed. My heart raced as I realized what was happening. But while we were praying I felt as if the Lord spoke to my heart and told me the baby would live. We were wheeled back into my wife's room, where a pastor from our church was waiting. I relayed the bad news and asked him to continue to pray.

The doctor arrived. He was dressed in a gown for surgery. From the tests that had been done he told us there was a 94 percent chance the baby was not going to live. He was ready to do an emergency cesarean to take the baby.

The ultrasound machine was brought into the hospital room and the doctor did one more check on the baby. But this time it was completely different. The baby moved! We could see him breathing, we could see his hands touching his face, and his legs were kicking. It was a miracle!

The nurse studied the monitor and instructed us to look at it. She showed us the relatively flat line that had registered for two hours. She then showed us the line after God had healed the baby. The line now looked like the seismic vibration of an earthquake!

This experience confirmed what I had believed by faith: that God does hear us in our darkest hour when we cry out to him. It also taught me that miracles do still happen.

"I walked away shocked!"

TERRI BRACY,
Licensed Minister, United Church of Christ

The brightly lit auditorium was packed. The band was warming up as the soundman tapped the first of a dozen microphones. The well-dressed people in the crowd greeted one another with hugs and enthusiastic hellos. As the music swelled, the beat picked up and all attention was drawn to the front. Hands clapped. Feet stomped. Voices rose in joyous celebration. An exit door opened, and the first of four pastors danced onto the stage, Bibles raised, singing songs of praise. The crowd was ready, and the room vibrated with the spirit of God.

It was a far different scene the night before as I sat weeping at my kitchen table. It was late. I had worked a long day and had come home to a dying marriage and a young son who needed Mommy. Homework, dinner, a bath, finally bedtime, and now it was quiet and I had to study for a Bible class. A glass of wine was out of the question, and without that, the day stayed with me.

This week's lesson was on the gifts of the Spirit. Corinthians taught that speaking in tongues was the least of the gifts, but you would never know that from the church I attended. Everyone spoke in tongues except me, and I wasn't sure I bought any of it. If you did not show evidence that you were baptized in the Holy Spirit by using a secret prayer language, did that mean you were not filled with the Spirit at all? The truth was, I was so distracted trying to figure out if others were faking it, that it got in the way of my own worship.

I sat at the kitchen table weeping, knowing that I was in the wrong place in more ways than one, but not knowing how to find the right place. "God, are you here? Are you real? I need to know. I need to feel you. I need to be sure." I need, I need, I need! How dare I! I am nothing. How dare I! I completed my lesson and finally poured that glass of wine. I buried my question deep within, and I got through the night.

When I awoke, I got my son off to school and went through the motions of another busy workday in a busy office in a busy city surrounded by busy people.

Still exhausted, I found myself in a converted gymnasium, hands raised, music vibrating my body, awaiting joy. The senior pastor hushed the crowd. "Who here has not been baptized in the Holy Spirit?" he asked. Few hands rose. Most of his flock were well trained and had long ago, and many times since, received the gift of tongues. Those of us who had not were well known. My best friend cut her eyes sharply toward me to let me know I could not hide. I did not slide lower into my seat. Instead, I sat taller, rigid. I was angry. "Make your way to the altar if you have not yet, and you will receive," intoned the pastor. How dare he! I would not! I did not believe for an instant that this was for me. I would not blindly follow nor would I pretend. "I'm out of here," I sputtered to my friend, "If I had known he was going to pull this crap, I would have stayed home!"

Several folks turned and looked at me. One of my teachers beckoned, "Come up, Terri, don't be afraid." Afraid? I wasn't afraid. I was livid! The tears started streaming from the corners of my eyes. My chin thrust out defiantly as I walked to the front of the church.

My teacher calmed me as she placed her hands on my shoulders and then pressed her lips to my ear and whispered, "Pray with me." I immediately felt a catch in the back of my throat. My mind seemed to separate from my spirit and I could observe myself. What was this? I could feel a bubbling up from somewhere deep inside and all of a sudden these bubbles became words—words I had never uttered before. It was as if my body was so full of them that there was no place for them to go but out of my mouth. For several minutes I watched. I listened. I experienced. And then I stopped.

I walked away shocked, literally shocked. It was as if I had been electrified. Halfway back to my seat I stopped, and I knew. The Holy Spirit had filled me up. God was alive and had revealed himself in me. The experience of the active presence of the living God meant I would never question it again. I also knew I would never again pray in tongues. I left that congregation shortly thereafter, knowing its fundamentalist ways were not my own. But I was forever changed by this encounter, and it has become a seminal moment for me. I am now a minister of the United Church of Christ.

"I prayed God would send a guardian angel to watch over him"

ANGIE BUTLER, *Office Manager*

I've always believed in the existence of God, but in February 1997 I was given confirmation that he does exist and that miracles do happen.

My father was forty-seven at the time and had suffered a massive stroke. He fell into a coma that lasted almost three weeks. When he awoke, he could not speak and didn't respond to questions. The doctor met with my mother and me and told us we needed to start looking for a "home" for him. He said there was very little chance my father would ever be anything more than a "vegetable." When I tried to protest and question, the doctor offered his apologies and said there really wasn't anything more he could do.

During this entire ordeal, I prayed all the time. I was at my wits' end thinking I'd lost my dad and that he would never know his first grandchild, whom I was pregnant with. I left the hospital in a haze. I prayed harder that night than I've ever prayed. I prayed specifically that God would send a guardian angel to watch over my father. I prayed so much that when I woke in the middle of the night to use the bathroom, I found I was still subconsciously praying.

After work the next day, I made the hour's drive to the hospital to see my father. I was still praying as I walked into his room. What I saw not only stopped me from praying—it stopped my breathing as well. There on the bulletin board above my father's left shoulder was a small golden angel. I immediately burst into tears, and as I did, my father opened his eyes and looked at me. I felt so full of joy I thought I might explode! I gave my father a hug and told him that I knew he was going to be all right. And, for the first time, he smiled. I knew in that instant that God was real and did listen to our prayers.

When I got home that night I spoke with my dad's sister on the phone. I told her the story of my prayer and the guardian angel and Dad smiling at me. She started sobbing. I asked her what was wrong. Didn't she understand what I was telling her? He was going to be okay.

She then told me that when she had gone to the hospital that morning, she'd had the strongest urge to go into the gift shop. She said she walked straight to the counter and grabbed an angel pin that was there. She had felt her sole purpose was to get that pin for my dad. She purchased it, brought it to his room, and put it on his bulletin board. By that point in her story we were both sobbing.

Months later, my dad left the hospital and was able to hold his first granddaughter on the day she was born. With physical therapy he was able to walk, talk, and even drive his car. He had an almost complete recovery and lived for another eight years.

"Stop the fire"

CHERYL LEHMAN, *Jewelry Store Owner*

I belong to a Spiritualist church in San Diego. Not only do Spiritualists believe that those in the body can communicate with those who have crossed over, they believe in the power of prayer—all kinds of prayer.

Every October in California, the Santa Ana winds blow hot off the desert. The humidity drops low, making the air comfortably dry and warm. For a few days the Santa Anas blow, and the skies from Ventura to San Diego become clear and blue—as God intended them. But blue skies don't smile for long. Inevitably they are replaced with billows of brownish-black smoke from wildfires throughout southern California.

October 2003 was no different. The dry winds were blowing and the temperature was in the nineties. A fire broke out early in the day at Camp Pendleton, north of San Diego. Then fires broke out northeast of Los Angeles and in San Diego County. Later that day there was another one in Riverside County. That night flames could be seen in San Bernardino and Fontana. All of a sudden it seemed as if all of southern California were on fire.

The fourth day after the fires started, a slim stream of white smoke emerged from the brush on the face of the mountain above San Bernardino, near my home. Surely the firefighters would come soon. I expected a helicopter bearing water from Lake Arrowhead to come and put out the fire. But no one came.

There was no one available to come. All the firefighters were working elsewhere. And the little stream of white smoke grew as the day wore on.

By dark, all electricity on the mountain was out. Flames were shooting through the darkness. The fire was spreading unabated. My husband and I left our home at 2 a.m. with our golden retriever, Max.

We stayed in a hotel at Big Bear while we called relatives and friends to see if we could come to them. But the fires were everywhere and we had to stay where we were, helpless.

Four days passed. The news told us everything. Fifty thousand homes, eighty thousand outbuildings, and two thousand businesses near our home in Lake Arrowhead were under attack from every direction. We watched the television intensely. We felt helpless and out of control. There was only one thing we could do—pray.

My husband and I had seen many instances when unfavorable circumstances had changed dramatically due to constant requests to God. We believed we could save our home if we petitioned him and his mighty angels. So the prayers began in earnest.

According to Spiritualism, we all have many spirits with us as well as an Indian guide. Indian guides can be our own ancestors, or people who are attracted to us through likeness, or someone assigned by God to protect us. When we learn their names, it makes it easier to communicate with them. My Indian guide's name is Sparkling Rain, and my husband's is North Wind. So during our prayer sessions we called on Sparkling Rain and North Wind to stop the fire and save our home.

The fires continued to rage. Then one night the television news showed pictures of the fire, and we recognized the location. It was just below our house.

All of a sudden the wind turned direction and started blowing from the north. And then it started to rain! And just like that, it was over. We returned to our home to find it standing like a tower of strength with burn lines all around it.

Our prayers had been answered. The North Wind had blown and the Sparkling Rain had fallen to put out the fire.

"All the pain was gone instantly!"

VANESSA FOSTER, *Airline Reservations Agent*

On a sunny, beautiful day in May 2005, I woke up with the urge to thank God that I was alive. I prayed and thanked God for continuing to bless me.

My husband and I were in the market for a new home, so I got into my van that day to go house hunting. As I headed north toward a nearby mall, I made a right-hand turn and lost control of the van. As I looked up, I saw that I was heading toward a steel bulldozer on a jobsite. I knew I was going to hit it and felt helpless. At that moment everything went quiet and I went into a trance. I felt as if I were falling through a tunnel in slow motion. When the van hit the bulldozer, I didn't feel anything.

I remember hearing the paramedics saying they thought my neck was broken. I could see myself lying on the ground and I could see them working on me. When I regained consciousness, I heard a man say I was one lucky person.

The ambulance came to take me to the hospital, and my neck wasn't broken. I felt that without a doubt God had spared my life.

But a month after the wreck I was in so much pain I could hardly walk. On top of that, all the pain medication made me feel like a zombie. I told my husband that if God had spared my life, he could heal my back from the pain I was experiencing. So I went to church, and at 10 p.m., I sat on the front bench and I prayed and spoke these very words to God, "God, I am so tired of taking this medication and I believe that at this very moment you can heal me. In the name of Jesus, I claim my healing and I am thanking you in advance. I will not take any more medicine." At that very moment, I felt a warm sensation go from the top of my back all the way down, and I jumped up. All the pain was gone instantly!

God is awesome, and my faith is stronger than ever before.

"Allow me to find some money"

CHARLES DIXON, *Writer/Gardener*

My third-grade math teacher gave us the class period to discuss any topic. God became the topic of conversation. She took a count of those in the class who believed in God and those who did not. I was one of the few who said I didn't believe in God. Really, I had never given the thought serious consideration.

After school that day my mother sent me to the corner store to buy a bottle of Kool-Aid. The store was about a half mile up the road. I purchased the Kool-Aid and started the walk home. Suddenly the conversation we had at school came to my mind. I said to myself, "If there really is a God, this is his opportunity to prove himself to me. Allow me to find some money in the road and I will believe."

The next step I found a fifty-cent piece. The next step another half-dollar. The next step another fifty cents. By now I had forgotten the request I had made to God. I continued to walk and collect the coins. Then suddenly I remembered. It terrified me to the point that I ran home as fast as any boy could, afraid to hold my head up, fearing I might see the presence or power responsible!

Once I got home, it took me some time to gather my composure. Finally I told my mother what had happened. She explained to me that someone must have had a hole in his pocket. It was just a coincidence.

I am fifty years old, and God is my all and all. All of my trust. All of my faith. All of my hope. God is my all and all.

"Don't you ever go forgettin' that"

BONNIE BAKER, *Retired Nurse's Aide*

Going to Grandma's house in Sunshine, Maine, was always a big adventure for me. Always delighted by my visits, she would help me cut out paper dolls from old catalogs or fetch the big box that contained old photographs of her five children. We would laugh together at the dresses and hairdos, and she would always come up with an amusing anecdote for each picture.

Grandma had her serious moments as well. After every meal we would read a chapter from her worn Bible and pray. I will never forget the morning Grandma asked God for a broom. Even in my childish reasoning, it seemed too small a thing to bother God with. However, I kept my thoughts to myself while Grandma cheerfully worked throughout the morning, scrubbing clothes on the washboard and eyeing the dust that needed to be swept away.

Outdoors in the sunshine, I soon forgot Grandma's prayer as I picked wild strawberries—popping them into my mouth to savor the juicy sweetness. So absorbed was I in my task that I didn't hear the footsteps on the graveled path. My head shot up as David, Grandma's neighbor, called my name.

"Is your grandmother inside?" he asked with a big, friendly smile. I nodded, my throat too constricted to speak. I watched as he strode up to the house, whistling and swinging a broom in his hand. Awestruck, I sat in the middle of my berry patch. Had God really sent Grandma a broom? A tiny seed of faith was planted in my heart as I pondered the miracle.

After David left, Grandma burst outside. "Lizella had an extra broom an' thought of me this mornin'," Gram said, referring to one of her close friends. "She sent it over by David." Her face beamed. "Isn't it a dandy?"

Inside, we knelt by the worn sofa to give thanks. Then Grandma went to work, whisking away all the dust until the house was spotless. Her crinkly blue eyes shone as she laid aside her broom and pulled me onto her apron-covered lap. "Child, don't ever be afraid of askin' God for what you need," she said, stroking my brown curls. "He really cares about us. Don't you ever go forgettin' that."

And I never did.

"I asked for a sign"

EVA HOUSER, *Personal Assistant*

For several years my life was in a downward spiral. My spirit was broken and all my faith was nearly gone. Everything I tried to do only seemed to make my life more miserable.

One day, when I could take no more, my life was turned around. I had been praying and could not imagine why God had not answered my prayers. After all, isn't that his job? Isn't he supposed to take care of us? One last time, I thought; I will try one last time. So I prayed, but this time my prayer was different. I didn't just ask him to fix things. I asked for his guidance to be proactive in my own life, to allow my eyes to see the answers he was laying in my path—answers I must be missing with my earthly eyes. Most important, I was bold! I asked for a sign. I asked for a sign I could see, feel, and use in my pursuit of a new and better life. I asked that this sign be placed directly in the palm of my hand so there would be no question as to whether it was a true sign or just a coincidence. I had prayed for hours and must have fallen asleep. When I woke, I was sobbing.

The next day went as usual. Out of bed early, off to work. It was nearly Christmas, and the very special woman I work with, Rosalind, had asked for my help wrapping gifts. As we worked away, we talked. I spoke briefly of my prayer the night before, but I was careful not to mention the sign I had requested, for fear she might think I was a little nuts. All of a sudden she left the room, and when she returned she didn't say a word. She just took my hand and placed not one but two prayer cards right in my palm! The cards were about praying to the Holy Spirit and turning my troubles over to him. This was what I had asked for! Tears started to flow as I exclaimed, "You have no idea what this means to me!"

"I WAS KICKING AND FIGHTING AND CLAWING"

Welcoming the Guardian

"I was in the center of a storm"

SENATOR DICK MOUNTJOY,
Retired California Senator and Assemblyman

In the fall of 1994 I found myself in a unique position. I had
served as a California state assemblyman for seventeen years
and was up for reelection when a seat in the state senate opened
up. I wanted to work in the senate and filed for the seat. Unfor-
tunately, a legal issue prevented me from dropping my bid for
the assembly, and I was forced to run for both positions simultaneously.

It was a tough, negative election. One and a half million
dollars was spent in a campaign to make sure I didn't get the
senate seat. But despite the campaign, I ended up winning both
seats.

The fact that I had two positions became an opportunity for
my party, the Republicans. In the assembly, the Republicans took
the majority in what was previously a Democrat-controlled house.
Their goal was to remove the Democratic Speaker of the House.
With my vote we could do it. I agreed to stay in the state assembly
until we voted to get rid of the Speaker, at which point I would re-
sign and go to the senate. I figured that would take a week.

But it didn't happen that way. One of the Republican assem-
blymen went against the party, and the vote to oust the Speaker
became a tie. The Speaker stayed.

What happened next was difficult and unexpected. The
tables turned on me. The Democrats in the assembly planned to
expel me from the assembly, while the senate began action to

nullify my election to the senate. If that happened, I would be out of office completely.

It was a time in my life when I knew I was doing the right thing, but I didn't know what was going to happen. I was in the center of a storm. It was like an emotional roller coaster. I couldn't focus on many things because of the turmoil in my mind. It was nerve-racking because I didn't know what my future would be.

I had been advised not to go near the capital, because if I was on-site, the Democrats could call a session and vote me out. Despite this threat, I decided to go. It was a busy day, and the rotunda was full of people. You could barely move. I was making my way across the room when, for some reason, I glanced at the north doors and saw a lady coming at an angle through the crowd. I made eye contact with her and had the feeling that she was coming toward me. She was a plain-looking woman with sand-colored hair and a soft face. She didn't have anything with her, not even a purse. She came right up to me and said, "What is your name?" I said, "My name is Dick." She replied, "I've been sent to pray for you. Can we pray right here?" And I found myself saying to her, "I think that's a good idea."

She put her hand on my shoulder, and in the crowded room she began to pray. I can't remember the things she said. People were moving all around us, and I remember thinking how amazing it was that no one was bumping into—or even touching—us. She was there for five minutes, and when she finished, she just turned and left. I didn't have a chance to say thank you or anything.

I finished my walk across the rotunda and started down the steps that went to my office. As I put my hand on the handrail, a sensation of warmth passed through my body. The feeling was similar to the effect you get from drinking liquor quickly. And with the sensation came a sense of peace.

I walked into my office, called my wife, and said, "There's nothing wrong anymore. Everything is going to be okay." I then told my chief of staff that all my worries had just disappeared.

A month of political wrangling passed and I was still feeling the same way—free of worries, even when the Speaker called a meeting to expel me from the state assembly. I went on the floor of the assembly that night. The newspaper reporters were there and were saying to me, "You don't look nervous for someone who's about to lose his seat in the legislature." My response was that everything would be okay. That night there was a vote, and the Democrats expelled me from the state assembly.

As I was heading home, I walked into the parking garage to get my car and the attendant told me I had a phone call. It was the president pro tem of the senate. He said, "You need to show up in the morning. We're going to install you in the state senate." They didn't nullify the election after all. The next day I was a senator.

From the moment this stranger prayed for me, nothing else was a concern. It was an unbelievable feeling. It was incredible. It was real. I'll never forget it. It made me thankful there is a God.

"A man stepped out of the van"

SARAH PIERSON,
Retired Radiographer/Mammographer

My twin daughters were eight years old when I took them to a school festival. When we arrived at the school, the parking lot was full, so I parked our minivan on the street. As I got out of the car, one of the girls started screaming. I ran around the car to see that her hand was caught in the sliding door of the van. Her sister had accidentally closed the door on her.

I tried desperately to get the door open, but it wouldn't move. I looked around for help. I was pulling and pulling and pulling, and the door wouldn't open. There was no one nearby—they were all at the festival. I was so panicked. I didn't want to leave her crying and in pain with her hand in the door, and yet I knew I had to leave her to get help.

Just as I was turning to run for help, the door popped open and a man stepped out of the van. He just climbed out and walked away. I don't know where he came from or how he got in the van without my seeing him. I started hugging my daughter, and he just walked past me without saying a thing. I didn't get his name or anything. He was just gone. That was it.

It was such a strange, surreal feeling. After it happened, I wanted so much to thank this mysterious man who appeared out of nowhere to help us. I now know that he was an angel or God himself in the disguise of a man.

"What are you looking for?"

JEFF KRIEGER, *Aerospace Manager*

I had just arrived for a business trip in Melbourne, Florida. It was my first time in this city. A group of us met in a hotel lobby and decided to reconvene at a specific restaurant ten minutes away. Since I was staying in a different hotel, I decided to drive my rental car separately to the restaurant.

But I soon discovered that the restaurant was not where I thought it was. I drove up and down the main drag for thirty minutes. I was very frustrated and angry with myself. I also felt embarrassed since my coworkers would all have been there by this point and probably would have ordered.

I was stopped at a traffic signal. It was dark and I was about to give up when, out of character for me, I said aloud, "God, please help me find this restaurant!" I then looked out the driver's-side window to my left, and in the car next to mine, also stopped at the light, was an old man waving his arms at me, trying to get my attention. I rolled down the window to see what he wanted. To my surprise, he asked me what I was looking for.

I told him I was looking for a barbecue restaurant but I couldn't even remember the name of it. He told me to turn right at the light and to follow him about half a mile and it would be on the left-hand side of the road. I did as I was told and, sure enough, he took me right to the restaurant, pointed out his window for me to turn into the parking lot, and waved good-bye.

I sat in the car for a minute or two to gather my thoughts before joining my coworkers inside. It certainly was confirmation to me that God will help if you ask.

It has been several years now, and I still recall this event as an example of how God works in our lives.

"I was kicking and fighting and clawing"

ANNE BARTON, *Substitute Teacher*

W hen I was fourteen, I went for a weekend trip to a place called Camp Warnecke on the river in New Braunfels, Texas, with my Spanish class. It had rained heavily the week before and the river was swollen and moving faster than normal. We all got in inner tubes and floated down the river, winding our way among the boulders and natural chutes. After floating downstream in the rapids, we would get out at a spot where the rocks ended, walk back to the starting point, and do it all over again.

After doing this several times, I asked my friend if she wanted to float through the chutes without inner tubes. She agreed and off we went, floating amid the rocks while being pushed by the current.

I was in the lead when I came to the end of the rapids and was spit out into the main part of the river, which was moving very quickly. I looked ahead and saw a fifty-foot-high concrete wall where the river was forced to turn. In front of the wall was a giant whirlpool, and before I knew it, I was in it and under. I was kicking and fighting and clawing to the surface with all my might. I don't know how long I was down when all of a sudden I felt something. I grabbed it, pulled up, and found myself in the middle of an inner tube. I looked around and saw no one except my friend, upstream from me, safely on a rock, crying. The tube seemed to have come out of nowhere.

I kicked my way back to the shore. When I got out of the water, I again looked to my left and then my right. No one was on the shore. About thirty feet ahead of me was a crowd of people. All of a sudden the crowd parted and a man walked out of it and came toward me. "That's my inner tube," he said calmly. "I was watching you and thought you might get into trouble. I had two inner tubes. I threw the first one and it missed you. I threw the next one and it landed over your hands."

I handed him the inner tube and said thank you, and he just turned and walked away, all by himself, disappearing into the crowd.

"Do the hard work for less money"

KATHRYN POINDEXTER, *Campaign Manager*

I was a senior in college with no idea what I was going to do after graduation. I had submitted some résumés and gone on some interviews and had had a very interesting job offer from a political nonprofit organization. But it was a hard job. I would be living in Washington, D.C., working campaign hours (at least seventy a week) for very little money. I didn't know if I could handle the work and such a small salary.

I postponed my decision to take the job and went to an interview for a plumbing company. The job would require fifty hours a week and pay about twice what the nonprofit would. But I would be selling plumbing supplies, something that seemed very boring to me.

As I sat at the human-resources presentation, I listened as the representative for the plumbing company talked about the hours and benefits. She kept repeating, "You've got to do the hard work for less money and it will pay off in the long run." She was recruiting people to take her plumbing jobs, but all I heard was "Work for the nonprofit." And I heard it over and over and over again.

I've often heard the saying "God speaks through other people," and that's what happened for me. I didn't hear the sound of anyone else's voice except hers, saying, "You 've got to do the hard work for less money," again and again. At that point I knew, in that still, small voice kind of way, that I should listen to what she was saying. I knew without question that her words were directed specifically toward me and I was being given an important message.

And so I listened to that voice and worked for the nonprofit. I started out poor and worked harder than I ever had. But because I listened to the message, I've been able to have a positive impact on the world that I wouldn't have had selling plumbing supplies.

I keep the plumbing company logo on my key chain to remind me there is a plan for my existence.

"God is inside you"

DAVE HURLEY, *Artist/Mental Health Worker*

I t was 1977 and I was in art school in New York City. It was a beautiful fall day and I was sitting on a park bench outside the school with a friend. My friend was unaware of it, but I was practicing a yoga breathing meditation while I was sitting there with her.

As I meditated, I followed my breath in and out of two energy centers, my crown and heart chakras. I would take a breath into my heart chakra, opening my heart to the universe, and send it out through my crown chakra, sending it up to God. And then I would do the opposite. I would draw on the Divine energy, taking it from God and sending it out as compassion. To be quite honest, most of the time it didn't work. But on this day, as I focused in the present moment, these centers opened up and I felt a state of grace that was incredibly simple. It was working.

My meditative state seemed to be attracting people to me. You know how happiness is contagious? It was like that. People we didn't know were coming up to us and talking. And then an older woman approached me from a busy sidewalk of passing pedestrians. Without any introduction, she walked right up to me, put one hand over my heart and the other on the top of my head, and began tapping quite forcefully with both hands, saying, "God is inside you. God is inside you." I laughed and asked, "How do you know God is inside me?" She then said, "I know. I know more than you think."

My friend was watching this exchange with a quizzical look on her face when the woman turned to her and said, "You don't have to worry. Your husband will take care of you." I responded back to her, "Yes, but doesn't a man need to be taken care of by his woman?" "Yes," she said, "your wife is taking care of you." "Oh, I have a wife?" "Yes," she answered, "you have a wife!" And then she walked away.

As it turns out, this stranger was right. I had just started dating a woman who turned out to be my wife. We recently celebrated our twenty-fifth wedding anniversary.

"He terrorized me"

KATHLEEN EBERLY, *Senior Pastor's Assistant*

Christmas 1992 was a very dark time for me. I was married to an active alcoholic who was extremely abusive. I worked full-time and my husband didn't work. At night he terrorized me by using guns and knives to threaten my life and the lives of my pets.

It had been a difficult year. I had lost some people close to me. My husband had killed one of my cats, and now my cat Bud was extremely sick and I knew in my heart my husband was to blame.

One evening I received word that my nephew had been in a very bad accident and had gone through the windshield of a car, losing part of his face. He was like a brother to me, and I rushed to the hospital to be by his side.

When I came home from the hospital, my husband told me Bud had died. That was the last straw. I lost it. I began destroying Christmas decorations and then ran outside into the snow and just sobbed. As I sat there crying my heart out, a woman appeared. I have no idea where she came from. She put her arms around me, and as she did, I felt a warmth I had never known.

She took me into the house, where she continued to comfort me. I told her what was happening in my life—how I blamed the death of my cat on my husband, and how I had to get out of the marriage or end my life.

She said I couldn't do either. She said God's plan included my husband. She said there were bigger plans in the works and that we had to stay together. She told me that taking my life was something I had to put totally out of my mind, that it wasn't what God wanted. She said I had to trust him.

This stranger also told me that Bud died so another cat could be helped and that I would have another cat within days. She said God knew how I loved animals and cared for them. She prayed with me, dried my tears, and left.

I had never seen this woman before and never have again. She told me she was taking a class nearby, but when I went to the place where she was to have been, nobody had ever heard of her. Was she a guardian angel? I think so.

That night was a turning point in my faith, when I became totally sure of God's love for me. I had listened to what that woman said to me, and I can see now why she gave me those messages.

As the woman had foretold, I did have another cat in my arms within days of meeting her. And despite the continuing abuse, I stayed with my husband. It was extremely difficult. But in staying, a miracle occurred. I had been told I could not have children. I was blessed with a beautiful son.

But the abuse continued and worsened. My husband developed cirrhosis of the liver and became very sick. He threatened me with a knife in front of our child, and not being able to take it any longer, I left my home and moved away. I took out a restraining order, but the threats continued.

And then one night when I didn't think I could handle another day of it, I cried out to God. I said, "I can't take this anymore. I surrender this all over to you."

The next day I learned that my husband had died. He had died as I had been crying out to God for help.

God has blessed me in so many ways since that night. If I hadn't stayed with my husband, I wouldn't have the wonderful child who is such a blessing to me. And today I work counseling women in my church. I am thankful for the suffering I experienced because without it, I would not be able to help others.

"No human being could disappear that fast"

ED CWYNAR, *Research Chemist*

Three weeks prior to my mom's death of a rare disease called amyloidosis, she sent me to the hospital pantry to get her some tea and ice cream. There were two nurses in the pantry and a patient, an older gentleman. He was hooked up to a movable rack with several bottles attached.

The nurses were in the back of the pantry heating up food in the microwave. I recognized them after having been there for four days and attempted to start up a conversation, but they ignored me. The man turned to me and began talking. He told me his name was Abner. We spoke for about three minutes before the nurses popped open the microwave door and left in a hurry with their food.

"Some people are just invisible to those living today," Abner said. I chuckled. He then told me he had been visiting my mother. We spoke for about ten minutes before he left.

When I got back to Mom, I mentioned Abner. I told her he said he'd stopped by to see her today and that it had been his fourth visit this week. I mentioned that he said he had known her since she was a kid. She had no clue who I was talking about and couldn't think of anyone she had ever known named Abner. A bit later I walked down the hall of cardiac and cancer patients, but I couldn't find him. I checked with the nurses a few days later to see if they had anyone on the floor with a first or last name of Abner. They didn't.

A week later Mom got worse. The amyloidosis began to penetrate her blood-brain barrier. Her oncologist had told me this would occur near the end of her life. Her communication skills diminished. We had to work on her language as she tried to communicate what she wanted. Each phrase she said actually meant something else.

One day in particular I spent seven hours translating and writing down her new "language." Exhausted, I decided to take a break before my brother arrived for his evening visit. I went back to the pantry to get some instant soup and something to drink. I was heating up the soup in the microwave when Abner showed up. I told him I had looked for him during the week but couldn't find him. "I had other friends to visit," he said, and paused. "I stopped by to see your mom every day, sometimes three times a day." "Who are you?" I asked. "Abner!" he responded. "I know your name is Abner," I said, "but who are you?"

At that moment he knew that I knew. I knew he was a heavenly spirit. "Your mom's only got a little time left . . . I don't know the exact time. Make her at peace. I took care of your mom when she was a kid. Now I'm here to take her home when she's ready." I reached for his arm and grabbed it. It felt like flesh and blood. "Now I know you're real," I said.

As he turned to leave, he struggled to get out the door with all the medical bags attached to the rack he was pushing. As the door began to close, I reached for it and left the pantry about a half second behind him. When I looked down the hall, he was nowhere to be seen and there was no sound coming from any direction. No human being could disappear that fast. I was right!

This experience reaffirmed my belief and pointed me in a different direction in my life. To me, it was God's reassurance that he wants me to be more spiritual and that my mortal health is not as important as my spiritual health.

"He forgot to let go"

LAURIE SWISTAK, *Elementary School Teacher*

It was September of 1986. My parents and I were at a mall with my sons—Patrick, who was almost three, and Brian, who was seven and a half. I took Brian into a toy store while my parents watched Patrick.

When I returned from the store, my parents were visibly shaken. With tears in his eyes, my dad told me what had just happened.

Patrick had been standing at the bottom of the escalator, moving his hands along the railing. At some point, he forgot to let go and the escalator carried him upward with his body hanging over the side.

Within seconds, my father was racing up the stairs to help him. By then, Patrick was halfway up the escalator, dangling twenty feet above a marble floor. Before my father could reach him, a woman, dressed in all black, reached over the side and pulled Patrick to safety. She then handed Patrick to my dad. As he held Patrick closely, he looked up to thank her, but she was gone.

When this happened, Patrick had just been scheduled for open-heart surgery to repair a hole in his heart. The surgery was going to be in November, and our hearts were very heavy with the terror of it as we prepared ourselves and Patrick for this upcoming ordeal. I think God knew I needed the affirmation that he was going to be okay—before the surgery.

My family had received the presence of God, powerfully, during the previous three years. I was diagnosed with a brain tumor when Patrick was five months old. Four months later my husband had a heart attack. The terror that came with the knowledge that we might lose our child required another affirmation of God's love and care for us. The incident with Patrick occurred before I even realized I might be faltering in belief and trust. Our Lord has a way of stopping us in our tracks and gently lifting our faces to him.

"YOUR FAITH HAS CURED YOU"

Receiving the Healing

"I began to see inside people"

TOM CLAUSEN, *Healer*

When I was twenty years old, I was in a serious car accident. I remember looking down from a place of love at a team of medical people frantically and roughly working on my lifeless body in an operating room. I seemed to be accompanied by a presence that I could not see but which was beautiful beyond words. I was being given a choice of staying or going back to my body when I received a message that there was more to do. When I regained consciousness a few days later, doctors told me I had died and was lucky to be alive.

I dismissed my experience as a dream until twenty-one years later, when something happened to me that changed my life forever. I was working as a training officer for a mining company when I decided to take a few days off to go prospecting. My father had taught me how to use a divining rod to search for underground water and minerals, and I had had success doing it. On this trip, I set up camp and headed out in search of gold.

I was following an old, overgrown wagon trail using my divining rods to guide the way when, *bang!*—I was zapped. It was like lightning striking in my head. There was a flash and an explosion. I was flattened and found myself sitting on the ground with the feeling of a huge weight holding me down.

I eventually found my way back to my campsite, where I slept for a week—getting up only for food and to use the toilet.

Each time I woke, I was consumed with the need to pray, to be totally absorbed in something to do with God. It was strange, because up until that moment I hadn't been interested in religion at all. I had some vague impression that there was a God somewhere in people because there was good in people, but it was a fairly shallow belief.

When I got back home with my family, I found I was still consumed by a powerful urge to fill my mind with prayer. I went to church, joined a men's prayer group, and studied the Bible. I couldn't get enough of it.

My job on the mine took the direction of looking after people—through training, safety, and first aid. I also began volunteering for a local football team to help injured players. Most of the time I just bandaged people up and gave them massages. And then something really strange happened. People started getting better before they should, and I had no idea why. I knew it wasn't me! I began to see inside people, the problems in their bodies and what was happening in their minds to cause them. Word got around, and pretty soon people were showing up at my home nearly every night and on weekends, asking me to treat their injuries.

I reached a point where I decided I had to find out what was going on with me. I left the country for the city. But I didn't find the answer. It wasn't until I finally came to a point where I said, "God, you've given this to me, so now you'll have to teach me," that I separated myself from other styles of healing and let the energy itself teach me.

My belief is that there is an energy. I hesitate to call it God, but there's an energy that is all-encompassing. It seems to be all knowledge, it seems to be all-guiding, and it seems to be everywhere. I live my total life in it.

After devoting the past eighteen years to allowing the healing energy to have its full expression through me, I have come to realize that amazing is normal. The many instances of incurable and unfixable things being healed—be it people, animals, land, weather, or whatever—have convinced me beyond a doubt that an energy, an energy of love, is available for humans.

"She refused to die"

MICHAEL TRUSLOVE, *Company Director*

My wife, Georgia, had been on medication for depression for forty years. The compounded effect of the drugs eventually affected her liver to the extent that her organs shut down. Her doctor advised me that she had suffered irreversible damage to her brain and other organs and that she had only a couple of hours to live.

I called our two sons, who would need to take a plane to get to us. We discussed whether they should come now or wait for the funeral. I began to prepare for the inevitable.

My mother spread the word around to all her friends, who were (unlike me) good churchgoing folk. Prayers were said at every church, synagogue, and mosque in the state. I believed in a noninterventionist God, but my mum felt otherwise.

As my wife lay unconscious in a hospital room set aside for "terminals," she refused to die. Ten days later she was discharged from the hospital. Her organs have all recovered and there is no brain damage.

I believe the collective prayers said for her by people of all religions—those who knew her and those who didn't—worked. Thank heavens I now have her back again, better than ever. I think maybe he thought I wouldn't be able to cope without her. He would've been right!

"A 10 percent chance of survival"

SARAH GREGSON, *Mother*

My baby was overdue by nine days. I wanted to have her naturally and had heard of a hospital that had birthing suites where you could do that. The suites had a policy that, if you were overdue, you had to come in first for a routine ultrasound to scan the placenta. My own doctor wouldn't be there, but I felt confident that everything was fine.

I arrived at the hospital, where they went ahead and scanned the placenta to see if it would last for a natural onset of labor. And then the radiographer decided to scan the baby. The second scan wasn't standard practice, but the radiographer wanted to do it because she hadn't seen me before. In doing this scan she discovered that there was a problem with the baby's heart.

A team of specialists was called to stand by. Labor was induced, and my daughter, Julia, arrived three hours later. She was immediately taken to the neonatal unit, where the cardiologist from the nearby children's hospital assessed her and ordered that she be transferred to his unit.

The surgeon called us into his office for the news. He told us she was in a bad state. She would need open-heart surgery for a valvotomy, and because of the critical nature of the problem, plus the added complication of a damaged left ventricle, she only had a 10 percent chance of survival.

We were devastated. Someone asked us if we wanted her baptized before the surgery and we went ahead and did it.

Within hours, there was a massive prayer circle from the United Kingdom to the United States and around Australia. We said a prayer as the doors to the operating room closed, and I can honestly say I felt enveloped in love and peace when I handed Julia over to God and the operating team.

The surgery went well, but the surgeon told us it would be up to Julia and the man upstairs as to whether she would pull through. Twelve hours later, Julia was out of the woods and the intensive care staff told us they had never seen such a miraculous recovery of the heart.

I believe God had his hand on Julia from the beginning, starting with compelling me to go to the birthing suite even though my own hospital was closer. The radiographer scanned her heart as a matter of interest. If the radiographer hadn't done that, the team of professional heart surgeons wouldn't have been standing by to help Julia. In the end, one circumstance after another ensured that a whole team of professionals was in the right place to help her.

Every day I thank God for what he did for Julia.

"A hellish world of drugs and prostitution"

DONNA MORALES, *Caregiver*

As a survivor of childhood incest, I was pretty messed up in my teens. It was a confusing time. I was sexually active at age fourteen and by sixteen had become infected with gonorrhea. I ended up in the hospital for a week with tubes in every orifice of my body because the infection was so bad. The doctor's words cut deep into my heart when he told me I was sterile and could never have a baby.

My life spiraled into a hellish world of drugs—and then prostitution to support my drug habit. I watched friends die from drug overdoses and bad trips on LSD. That was enough to scare me straight to rehab. I went cold turkey.

I came out of drug rehab and became an alcoholic. Life wasn't any better. By eighteen and a half I believed that life was worthless, and I made a serious attempt at suicide by jumping out of a speeding car.

Two years later, something was terribly wrong with me. I was sick to my stomach and was suffering from a host of other things. I made an appointment with the doctor who had treated me for the gonorrhea, because he had also told me that the disease put me at high risk for getting cervical cancer. I was only twenty years old and I thought my life was ending.

Dr. Katz did several tests and came into the room with my chart in his hand looking confused. He looked up at me and said, "Donna, you're pregnant!"

On my way home I went into three churches and cried my eyes out with happiness. I felt God had forgiven me for all the wrongs I'd done in my life.

My older son is thirty-six years old, my younger son is twenty-seven, and I have a seventeen-year-old daughter! The best blessings of all are the three grandchildren who came from my miracle babies!

"Run over by a truck"

FELICE IZZARELLI, *Spiritual Counselor*

I t was the day before my son Joseph's twelfth birthday, and he was outside playing with his friends in the street. I was inside the house reading the St. Francis prayer when I heard a *thump-thump*. I didn't know what it was until the kids came running to the door to tell me that Joseph had been run over by a truck.

When I first saw my son lying in the street, my only thought was "God, my son is in your hands." I kept saying, "Thy will be done," over and over again in my mind.

Both the front and back tires of the truck had gone over Joseph's stomach. His head had hit and dented the bottom panel of the truck. His ankle had hit a piece of metal under the truck, which had taken out a silver dollar–size chunk of his flesh, exposing the bone.

One of my neighbors had been looking out his window when it happened. This neighbor had already tied his belt around Joseph's ankle to stop the bleeding and had elevated his foot by putting it on a bucket. I didn't think it was a coincidence that this man was helping at the scene. God always sends someone where there is need.

I stayed with Joseph, asking for prayers of healing, and then ran to take care of the gentleman who had accidentally run over my son, asking for prayers for him.

Up until this point in my life I had wondered what would be the worst thing that could ever happen to me. I had always thought that if something happened to my son, I wouldn't be able to make it. Now I found myself saying to my Heavenly Father, "If this is your choice, then thy will be done and I will be okay with it." That was the hardest thing I'd ever had to do in my life!

The trauma team was waiting at the hospital and gave Joseph the best care. A CAT scan and X-rays found no broken bones and no internal damage—only tire marks across his stomach in the form of black-and-blue bruises. The hole in his leg had just missed the main artery. He would need a skin graft later on, but he was alive. After five minutes of healing by the laying on of hands, the bruises were gone and only the tire marks were left. It was a miracle.

The next morning my son woke up singing "Happy Birthday" to himself. Thank you, God! I know there were many prayers sent out that day for healing Joseph. The doctors were surprised at how fast he was healing. I wasn't. I knew it was God's healing power that was at work. In the end, Joseph didn't need a skin graft, and he's in perfect health today.

This experience made me realize how much we are a part of one another in a time of need. Everyone came to my aid: neighbors, doctors, paramedics, the fire department, and all those sending prayers. God bless them all. It also taught me a valuable lesson. I'd always had a fear of how I would react if something happened to my son. Now that fear has been removed and has been replaced by love, courage, and the strength of God to face all things in life.

"Your faith has cured you"

JACK GROSE, *Maintenance Technician*

My wife, Lesa, had been suffering from heart problems since her late twenties. In college she experienced fainting spells during which her heart raced to two hundred beats a minute. In her thirties she received a pacemaker, and we thought that would solve the problems. She was ready to get on with life and enjoy living again. But this was not to be. By thirty-five she had suffered the first of three heart attacks.

In August 1999 she was diagnosed with vasospasms of the heart, a genetic defect that had claimed other family members. In this condition, the arteries of the heart spasm and restrict blood flow. In Lesa's case, all the arteries on the left side of her heart were involved. The doctor told us this was a rare condition. He hoped medicine would help, but it wasn't a cure. He then warned us that the episodes would become more frequent and severe until one would take her.

Seven years later, I prepared for the inevitable. Lesa was in the critical care unit of the hospital—the same unit she worked in as a nurse—for the second time in a month. She was only forty years old. The doctor who had diagnosed her with vasospasms had been correct. Her spasms had become more frequent and more severe. She was on nitroglycerin to open the arteries and morphine for the pain. As I sat with her over a twenty-four-hour period, I watched as she received eighteen injections of morphine and over 100 micrograms an hour of nitroglycerin—the equivalent of putting fifty nitroglycerine tablets under the tongue each hour.

The senior cardiologist had been away on vacation when he walked in to see Lesa in this state. He felt time was getting short for her, but luckily he didn't just want to keep her comfortable—he wanted to do something. He saw Lesa a dozen times that day, conferred with other doctors, and read all he could find on her condition. He then ordered her transfer to the Indiana Heart Hospital in Indianapolis for a heart catheterization, a test to see what was going on and whether anything could be done to fix it.

Lesa was transferred to the hospital, and soon a nurse and an orderly arrived to take her into the operating room. Lesa's friend Brenda said a prayer over her, and I told her that I loved her and would be seeing her again. We were told the surgery could take up to twelve hours.

After an hour and a half, the doctor came into the waiting room, calling my name. I thought for sure the worst had happened because it was way too soon. He said we needed to talk, and I thought he was going to have me make a life-or-death decision. He then asked our family and friends to go back to Lesa's room. When I walked in, I got a surprise I'll never forget. My wife was sitting up in bed smiling at me.

The doctor informed us that he had tried very aggressively to get Lesa's heart to spasm, but the arteries would not do anything. They reacted like those in a normal heart. He told us her heart was 100 percent perfect! This was the same doctor who had seen her before. He had compared her previous heart catheterization pictures to the ones he had just completed and found they were nothing alike. Lesa's friend Brenda asked how this could be. Lesa had been on all that nitroglycerin—something that would have caused her extreme headaches if she didn't have something wrong with her—and now her heart was perfect?

The doctor had no answer. That's when Brenda said, "This has got to be Divine intervention."

My own first thought was that this doctor was mistaken in his diagnosis and findings. But sitting in front of me, obviously pain-free, was my wife. She was not on nitroglycerin or morphine. I walked out of the room to talk to the doctor. He again stated that all the previous catheterizations had shown severe problems, but that now all her arteries appeared normal.

I returned to Lesa's room more confused than ever. I asked her how she was doing, and she replied, "Great." She wanted to get up to use the bathroom. I told her I would get her a bedside commode, but she insisted on getting out of bed and walking to the bathroom. I waited for the pain to hit her. It never happened. No pain at all!

It was then that she told us what had happened. She said that while she was being taken to the operating room, she started praying that she would be healed. She said that all at once it felt as if her body was in a tub of hot water, and a great feeling of peace came over her. She said she felt the presence of God and that she knew then that everything was going to be all right.

Two days later we learned that at the exact time Lesa was going into surgery, one of her friends had e-mailed another with a verse from Matthew 9:22: "And Jesus turned and saw her and said, take courage, daughter; your faith has cured you. And the woman was restored to health from that moment."

Today Lesa is a full-time critical care nurse. We ride motorcycles together and play with our dogs. She's on a softball team and plays paintball every chance she gets. She's doing just great! There's not a doubt in my mind that her recovery was a miracle.

"SOMETHING TOLD ME NOT TO TAKE THAT FLIGHT"

Accepting the Warning

"The Crock-Pot was burning the wall!"

CATHERINE HOOD, *Real Estate Appraiser*

It was 1994 and my husband and I were living in a small one-bedroom condominium in New Jersey. I had never used a Crock-Pot but decided to try the one we had received as a wedding present to make a special dinner for my husband. I set it up on the kitchen counter in the morning, prepared the food, turned it on, and left it to do its cooking, which would take most of the day. I checked on it periodically.

Sometime after noon I was feeling tired and decided to take a nap on the couch. Just when I was in a comfortable sleep, I was abruptly awakened by the sound of emergency vehicle sirens. They were screaming to a halt just outside my front door. I jumped up, raced to the door, and opened it. I looked around but there was nothing—no police cars, fire engines, or ambulances. But I knew I had heard the sirens, and they were loud.

I turned around and looked into the kitchen. The Crock-Pot was burning the wall!

If I hadn't heard those sirens, the apartment could have burned down. I can't logically explain what happened, but it did.

The experience has left me with an incredible sense of security and well-being knowing that someone or something greater is watching over me.

"I went into a spin"

JEAN SHARP,
Health Care Communications Consultant

I live in the most western part of New Jersey and commute east to work every day, usually driving into New York City or my office, located about an hour's drive from my home. East and west New Jersey are connected by Route 78. It's a fairly benign highway during the noncommute hours, a treacherous one otherwise.

It was about ten o'clock on a beautiful fall morning as I made the commute. I wasn't in a rush. I was at peace with the lack of traffic and timeline and, uncharacteristically, stayed in the far right lane within the speed limit.

Suddenly I felt a very light bump to the back of my car, and immediately I went into a spin. My first concern was for the cars behind me. Would they be able to avoid colliding as I spun around the highway? I reached out to God and asked that I be spared a handicapped life. I would rather take the next step than that.

I found myself traveling backward, attached to the side of the truck that had hit me. My driver's-side door broke off as my car moved at sixty miles an hour in reverse with no brakes or any other control.

Still traveling in reverse, the car veered into the woodsy highway divider, went down a hill, and finally hit a tree. I waited for the gas tank to explode. It didn't. I shook my head in disbelief as I got out of the car. I was completely unscathed (except for a later case of poison ivy from the leaves that filled my car). I remember many people coming down through the woods to find me. State troopers and the travelers who witnessed the accident couldn't believe I had survived without a scratch.

During each step of this incident I remained conscious of the relationship between my survival and my connection with God. I have never been more connected to God than that day. I don't know why it was not my time, but I do know that God kept me here to do something. Maybe sharing this story for the first time is the beginning of this journey.

"We had no cash and no way of feeding the boys"

JANET DREWETT, *Career Development Consultant*

My husband and I were 24/7 house parents in a hostel set up for twenty Aboriginal schoolboys who lived in the city to attend high school. We were paid modest wages by a private organization, while the building and its contents were owned and maintained by the government.

Teenage boys are always hungry, and we lived week to week with just enough food to get by. I cooked everything from scratch and was completely dependent on the stove to feed the boys. One morning the stove broke down, so I was only able to give them tea and toast for breakfast. The maintenance people came, looked at the stove, and then took it away, saying they didn't think it would be back for at least two days. Without a stove, we were in trouble. I only had staples in the cupboard. We had no cash and no way of feeding the boys properly, so we prayed. We didn't tell anyone of our predicament—we just prayed.

The boys got home from school and it was tea and toast again, as I had not been able to bake. The boys hovered anxiously. There wasn't anything cooking on the stove, and we couldn't tell them what—or even if—we would be eating. Nevertheless, we set the tables as usual and around the time we normally served the evening meal, the doorbell rang. It was several ladies from the city Baptist church. They were carrying boxes of food from a convention they had had that day.

They said they had no idea why they had overcatered until we told them about the stove. There was more than enough food for a full evening meal and for lunches the next day. Another miracle was that the stove was returned the next day.

"I had a stash of sleeping pills"

MARILYN LAWRANCE, *Mother*

It was 1987. I was going through what I can only describe as the most harrowing, stressful, and grief-stricken period in my entire life. My marriage of twenty years had ended, and all the betrayals and deceits of the previous years had come to my attention. I felt that life was not worth living, and the only escape I could see from the intense pain was to die.

My two children were uppermost in my mind at all times, and I knew that as a Catholic I should never take my own life. I begged and pleaded with God to help me, but I felt betrayed by him too.

I had a stash of sleeping pills, and on two occasions, around midnight, I was about to end it all when each time a different visitor came to my door. Both people told me they had received an urgent message from God to get to me. When they arrived and told me why they had come, I truly felt God was with me.

Never before or since have I had visitors to my door after midnight. God does exist, and he listens. He saved me.

"Stop buying them!"

BILL NICHOLLS, *Retired Carpenter*

My father died of lung cancer when he was sixty years old. Everyone in my family smoked. I was twenty-three when I started. By the time I was thirty-seven, I was smoking fifty cigarettes a day. To get to sleep every night I had to drink cough syrup to clear the phlegm from my lungs. I had tried to quit smoking many times, but I knew I would eventually be another cancer victim.

One night I decided to see if God was real. I went into a bedroom, locked the door, drew the curtains, and, feeling absolutely silly, got on my knees and said, "God, if you exist, I need to pack up smoking before it kills me." Immediately a strong thought was conveyed to me like an idea that just sprang into my head: "*Stop buying them!*"

I went into the kitchen and told my wife, Anne, what had just happened. Divine intervention is one thing, but cutting my habit from fifty a day to nothing? I thought on it for one week and decided to seek God's wisdom again. Maybe he would tell me to cut them down over a six-month period. So, same place again on my knees, but before I could say a word, it came again: "*Stop buying them!*"

Once more I informed Anne. This time she said, "So what are you going to do about it?" I told her that I'd have to go ahead and stop buying cigarettes.

Each day my morning ritual was to go to a local shop on my way to work and buy the newspaper and twenty-five Winfield Blues. The morning after getting the second message, I crossed the street early to avoid the shop owner, as I didn't really want to have to explain to him my Divine mission to stop smoking.

A week later, I was tempted. A friend left a pack of cigarettes in the open, and I couldn't resist trying one to see what it tasted like. I smoked the cigarette and immediately felt ill. I went to the nurse's station at work. I was nauseous and dizzy and had the sweats. I also felt as though someone had given me a smack over the head.

I have never smoked a cigarette since that day. It had nothing to do with willpower. The urge to smoke was taken away from me as if I had never smoked before. Years later, I came across a Bible verse that stated, "God rewards those who seek him." Indeed he did!

"All I saw were blinding headlights"

LEE HOWARD, *Nurse Manager*

When I was eighteen years old, I was driving home from work at around 2 a.m. when a car came at me head-on. All I saw were blinding headlights. I let go of the wheel and thought, "There's no chance I'm not going to be hit." I had a sense of darkness all around me and I blacked out.

When I came to, I was several miles from where I had been, and I couldn't believe I was safe. I had an overwhelming sense of not believing I was actually alive.

To this day, I know that Jesus took the wheel for me and kept me safe. I believe in Divine intervention and I know that we all come here with a purpose. I guess God isn't done with me yet.

"Drinking and driving"

GREGG MADZI, *Marketing Account Manager*

I was about eighteen years old and was driving home from a girlfriend's house after having too much to drink. I wasn't a big drinker, but on this night I was young and dumb.

I fell asleep at the wheel. When I awoke, I was heading straight for an eighteen-wheeler truck parked in my neighborhood on the opposite side of the road. I was within a few feet of the truck in the wrong lane. Startled, I turned the wheel to the right to avoid hitting the truck head-on. I will never forget the feeling I had as I turned my steering wheel to the right and the car turned left. I ended up parallel to the truck, facing the opposite direction from the way I was going.

Had the car turned the way it was supposed to, I would have taken out the entire driver's-side back end of my mother's Oldsmobile. I just sat in the car for a few moments, thanking God.

From this experience I learned a valuable lesson about drinking and driving. And at this point in my life I realized I no longer needed to depend on faith—I *knew* God existed. The irony of this story is that I am married to a wonderful woman named Sandy who is in a wheelchair because she was hit by a drunk driver when she was young.

"We would have all drowned"

HUGH CONWAY, *Construction Equipment Salesman*

L ate one Friday night some friends and I were driving up to our favorite swimming hole, a bottomless rock quarry in Bakerton, West Virginia. The quarry had sheer cliffs all around it, and the only way you could go swimming was to jump off a fifty-foot cliff into the water. You then had to climb up the cliff to jump again.

We had been partying most of the night, so we were all pretty hammered. My friend Mark was driving—he was the only one of us who had a car. He drove like a maniac when he was sober, so you can only imagine how he drove when he was high.

The quarry was entered through old farm fields. There weren't any access roads to it. On this particular night, it was very dark, and we had a lot of trouble finding the gate. When we did, Mark drove through it and into an old cow pasture. He then floored the accelerator and we went spinning and sliding all over the field. Mark enjoyed terrorizing us and would not stop even as his girlfriend, Nancy, and my friend Jim and I pleaded with him. Even now I have to admit it was fun.

After about fifteen minutes of Mark's doing this, all the while dodging boulders and trees, something happened. I screamed out as loudly as I could for him to stop. He hit his brakes and the car slid sideways for twenty feet until it finally stopped.

I was sitting in the front seat and when I looked out, I could see the edge of the quarry and a black void in front of us. The car had stopped inches before falling over the cliff.

If I had opened my door, I would have fallen in. We all had to get out of the car on the left side. If we had driven over that cliff, I know we would have all drowned and our families would never have found out what happened to us. We all just sat on the ground in shock and instantly sober.

I still don't know why I yelled the way I did, when I did. I feel that God spoke through me. To this day, my friend Jim remembers this as the time I saved his life. I remember it as the time God saved us all.

"A sea of shards of glass"

PATRICIA FRUTTAURO, *Jeweler*

My son was giving a lunch party for the family in the garden of his home in London. As we entered through the hallway, he said, "Look out for that mirror." It was a very long glass mirror that had been made to cover the full length of the hallway, to make it look larger. It was enormous. The mirror, we were told, had been delivered the day before and was propped in the hallway until it could be installed the next day.

We went into the garden, which was quite large, and people enjoyed drinks while my son barbecued. It was a very warm, sunny day, and Eleanor, my two-year-old granddaughter, was wearing a little sleeveless top and cotton pants as she played in the garden around us. We weren't really aware that Eleanor had detached herself until we heard a tremendous, horrific sound of glass breaking and Eleanor screaming.

My daughter and I were first on the scene. Eleanor was standing in the middle of a sea of shards of glass. We lifted her out, took her to the bathroom, and quickly undressed her to make sure she wasn't injured. There wasn't one mark on her, not one. But when we went back into the hallway to look at the scene, the passage full of glass, we found one of Eleanor's blond curls right in the middle of all that glass. The glass had somehow cut one of her curls off her head as it came down around her.

We all thought it was quite miraculous. It made people very quiet—reflective, really—because it was such an extraordinary thing. I remember thinking, "Oh, she has a guardian angel."

I tend to be a rather rational person, so I went through my mind thinking, "How could that have happened—the curl's being cut from her head without her being hurt?" I believe in a strength above us. I believe God stretched out his hand and protected Eleanor that day.

"Something told me not to take that flight"

BRUCE BRAMHILL,
Retired Diagnostic Image Technology Distributor

I t was February 24, 1989, and I was in Los Angeles on business. I was checking in at LAX to come back to my home in Melbourne, Australia. Just as I was standing there, a thought flashed through my mind: "Don't go back to Australia. Go to Switzerland." The urge was overwhelming. I just heard, "Don't get on that plane. Go in the other direction." It freaked me out. I'm rigorous and disciplined about how I travel, and I don't change my travel plans. But I turned around, booked a flight to Zurich, and made plans for a business meeting there.

When I disembarked in Zurich, I walked past a newsstand and noticed a photograph on the front of a newspaper of a United Airlines 747 with its front right-side door pointing straight up in the air. It was my flight. The cargo door had blown out over Hawaii, along with part of the fuselage and interior. Nine people were killed. My seat, the aisle seat in the front row of business class on the right side of the plane, remained, and those directly behind it were gone.

For me it was a very solid tap on the shoulder from the Great Spirit, telling me to do something different from what I had planned. More and more and more I now listen to those taps on the shoulder.

"Every single dart hit the bull's-eye"

PAULINE RICK, Missionary

A t thirty-two I had reached a point where I should have been content with my life, career, and international travel opportunities, but I wasn't. Friends were encouraging me to take a break from my life to search for God's direction by attending a five-month discipleship school.

I thought about it but was torn. I didn't want to leave my elderly parents, whom I lived with. I had a five-year relationship with my boyfriend (and didn't want to leave him), and I felt my brother needed my friendship and attention. I prayed and told God those were my three obstacles in terms of attending school.

Within three weeks my obstacles were removed. My parents decided to go to Chile to visit my sister. My brother took a job working and living on a sailboat. And my boyfriend came over one night and told me he'd accepted a job in another state and would be leaving in a few weeks.

A few months later, while I continued to toy with the idea of going to the discipleship school, a friend invited me to a pub where he played darts on Friday nights. I went along just for something to do. I had never really played darts before and I gave it a try. Naturally, I wasn't very good at it.

There was a man who played darts every Friday who *was* very good at it. He traveled to dart competitions around the state and always won. He had another interest. He wanted to get to know me better. I began to think it wasn't such a good idea to leave for school. I wondered if perhaps I should stay and pursue a relationship with him. He seemed very nice and interesting.

So one Friday night I was invited to team up with a friend and play darts against this man. It was now the fifth or sixth time I had played. I threw the first dart and it hit the bull's-eye. And then every single dart I threw hit the bull's-eye. It was as though the darts were going off to the side and then correcting to the middle. I thought it was a quirk of luck, but it continued each time I threw.

To me it was just a game, but to the dart guy this was serious business! This man I had thought was so sweet was getting angrier with each dart I threw. He accused me of being a professional dart player. He even called me a dart shark! He yelled at me until I grabbed my purse and left, nearly in tears.

On the way home I thought about how I had misjudged his character and how grateful I was to have seen how he reacted, making it clear to me he wasn't someone I wanted to be involved with. It occurred to me that God had intervened and caused those darts to veer off course and hit the center—something impossible for me to do. It was clear to me that God was directing me to leave the area and pursue school.

That was in 1992. I went to school and joined an organization called Mercy Ships, which operates hospitals on boats and brings medical attention to the poor in developing countries. I have always been grateful to God for pursuing me and guiding me from my silly ways.

"Please stop the rain"

ADELE DAVEY, *Retired Midwife*

My husband was building an extension to our house and was using an electric drill when it started to rain. He looked skyward and implored, "I need to finish the job. Please stop the rain." When the rain instantly stopped, we were surprised but didn't think too much of it until a bit later when my husband finished using the drill. He again looked skyward and said, "Thanks very much. You can let it go again," and immediately the rain started again. I looked at him and said, "Oh my God," and we burst out laughing.

It's been more than twenty-six years since that happened, and we still talk about the day the rain stopped and started again.

"She had lost all five of her kids"

FRANCINE WILLIAMS, *Retired Check Processor, Federal Reserve Bank*

I n 1972 I awoke one morning after a scary dream. In the dream a woman was sitting on a curb with her back to me. She was rocking and crying. I asked someone standing next to me what had happened to her and they told me she had lost all five of her kids—they had been killed. She was just crying so hard.

That morning, school was canceled because we had had a snowstorm overnight. My girls (I have five) wanted to go outside and play in the snow before breakfast. And although I had let them do this on many occasions before, for some reason I was adamant that they have breakfast before going out.

As they were eating, I walked to the front door to look out at the snow. I was standing in the doorway when my neighbor shouted for me to get back. I started to ask him why when the roof crashed down on the porch. Instantaneously, the pillars holding up the porch blew clear across the street and the porch tore away from the house! When the emergency services arrived, they thought there had been a gas explosion.

Had I let my girls go out and play instead of eating their breakfast, they could have been killed. Do I believe the dream was a warning from God that something was going to happen and I needed to protect my children? Yes I do!

"WHAT WAS THAT?"

Feeling the Light

"Fear began to fill my body"

MARK MONTGOMERY, *Retired Businessman*

May 21, 1968. 2 a.m. Da Nang, Vietnam.

I had been in-country forty-five days and hadn't seen any action. I was assigned the job of security guard for a compound next to the Da Nang River at a point where equipment, supplies, and troops were loaded and unloaded. The U.S. military also operated a ferry for civilians there.

As I stood ready in flak jacket, helmet, M16, and night flares, my field radio squawked. It was the front command post advising incoming rockets and ordering complete blackout conditions.

I was twenty feet up in a sandbagged tower, so I felt safe and had a good view. As a young man I was ready for action and confident I could handle it. How terribly wrong I was.

The first rocket landed far south of me with a soft thud. As the pattern was laid down, climbing toward me, the rockets became louder, associated with bright flashes of exploding gunpowder.

A lower tower about two hundred yards south of me took a direct hit and disappeared, along with the GI in it. Fear began to fill my body and I couldn't stop it. A second rocket hit a landing craft utility docked off the pier to my right, and the Vietnamese guard who was standing on it disappeared.

By now I felt two parts of myself: my body that was frozen like granite, and my fearful soul trapped inside it. As urine ran down my leg into my boot, my soul screamed out to God to save me. Just then I heard a male voice, off to my left and far away, softly saying, "I'm coming, I'm coming."

I couldn't understand why he was taking so long to get to me when I was in such dire need. And then I felt his spirit enter through the top of my body and slowly pour itself downward, exiting through my feet. Then I heard, "I am he; I am all there ever was or ever will be." He then told me he had always known me. He sprinkled my life before me. I saw myself as a two-year-old, then at five, then at eight, and I smiled as I felt like the little boy I was looking at. He then spoke the most potent words I have ever heard. He said, "I love you." The tears poured from my eyes. At that point I remember begging him to take me with him. I was only twenty-two, but I wanted to spend the rest of my life with him. I received no answer and felt him slowly leave me in the same direction he had come from.

As I looked around, I hadn't gone anywhere, but I knew I had somehow been taken out of my presence of mind to share an experience with the Holy Father, who indeed had saved me.

"Hand of God!"

STEVEN FOSS,

U.S. Military Reserve/Law Enforcement Officer

July 2005. Tall'Afar, Iraq. Combat Engineer Actions, 3rd Armored Calvary Regiment.

During what I thought was a lull in action as we conducted a raid into an enemy-held neighborhood, I stood exposed along a city street. It was stupid, I know. As I stood there, a firefight erupted from an alleyway half a block away and, yes, I continued to stand there.

I was intent on assessing the situation for the possible commitment of my soldiers in support when out of the corner of my eye a bright flash occurred and the pavement about eight meters to my front left exploded. A cloud of dust and debris blew across the street and enveloped me. At the flash, I ducked my head into my chest and listened. I felt myself being struck by numerous pieces of debris. "I'm hit!" The concussion knocked me back, but as the cloud of gas and debris dissipated, I found I was still standing, beaten and covered with grime.

I shouted out to my soldiers for an injury report and began a frantic pat-down in the areas of my body that were impacted and where I felt pain. I made a 360-degree look-around and noticed the Fox Troop mortar platoon guys nearby. They had witnessed the whole thing, including my post-blast antics. As they realized I hadn't sustained an injury, they began waving at me—some pointed, others laughed—as they shouted, "Hand of God, engineer! Hand of God!"

In Iraq, a country where the Bible comes to life right in front of you, I can only believe that my God's purpose is still not realized here. I will walk this path and address those things that he puts before me for the greater good of those who know me and those who do not except through the grace of his works through me.

"God carried me the rest of the way down the steps"

TAMMY BABCOCK,

University Honors Program Assistant

I was about twelve years old and home sick from school with the flu. My bedroom was located on the second floor of our house. When I got up in the morning, I decided to go downstairs to lie on the couch and watch TV. I was halfway down a fourteen-step staircase when I became dizzy and tripped.

The next thing I knew, I was standing upright at the bottom of the steps. I hadn't fallen. I remember thinking, "How did I get here?" The feeling I had was that I had floated, or had been gently delivered.

Someone—I feel it was God—had carried me the rest of the way down those steps. I did pass out and would have tumbled all the way down and could have broken my neck.

I am now forty-eight years old, and I remember it as if it were yesterday.

"I knew I had little chance of survival"

THEODORE KARLSEN,
Retired Marine Corps Master Sergeant

The year was 1947. I was six years old. My father was a logger in Oregon, and we lived well into the old-growth forest in the Oregon mountains at the end of a long logging road. Our home was a log cabin. Two fifty-gallon drums welded together provided the heat in our home. The top drum was used for cooking and baking. We burned wood in the bottom drum, and that heated the entire cabin. All five of us young kids climbed a ladder each night and slept together in a loft. We didn't have indoor plumbing. But we did have one absolute rule. We were always to do our business before dark since cougars were numerous in the area.

One night, when we were returning home very late, the car slid off the road and went down a steep embankment. We were about half a mile from our cabin but close enough to walk the rest of the way home. So we started to walk. About halfway, my father remembered he had forgotten something in the car and told me to return by myself to retrieve it.

I went back, retrieved the item, and started walking toward home. About halfway, I heard a limb crack to my left. The next moment, I heard the low, deep growl of what I was sure had to be exactly what I feared most, a cougar. Fear filled me like water being poured into a glass, and I knew I had little chance of survival. I was a dead six-year-old walking, and I knew it.

Then it happened. I felt engulfed by a warm blanket of light, though not a light as we understand light. It made me feel safe and secure, impenetrable as far as any danger was concerned. I could sense a presence of some kind. I just knew there was something protecting me and that nothing could harm me. All fear poured back out of my body.

At the time, I didn't understand what it was that saved me, but today I am convinced it was the very angel of God.

"What was that?"

CHERYL CRAMER, *Sales Representative*

I was nineteen years old when I left my home in Pennsylvania on a vacation to visit my sister and her husband in St. Petersburg, Florida. One day my sister suggested I go for a bike ride with my brother-in-law and take her bike. I had never ridden a bike other than my own. Hers was much taller than mine, and when I was seated, my feet didn't reach the ground. I figured it didn't matter since I'd be riding most of the time. So off my brother-in-law and I went.

After riding for about half a mile, we came to a stoplight. I put on my brakes and put my feet down, forgetting they wouldn't touch the bottom. As my feet hung in the air, I started falling over. All of a sudden, I felt two hands, one supporting my head and the other supporting my hip, slowing my fall to what felt like slow motion. When I reached the ground, the hand at my head moved to support my cheek while the other stayed on my hip and ever so gently let me fall softly to the ground. At that moment, my brother-in-law said, "What was that?" I looked up at him staring down at me. The hands disappeared. I got up, dusted myself off, and got back on the bike.

I believe God is all-powerful and all love. I know those hands were the hands of God or an angel. My brother-in-law's exclamation after seeing me go down in extra slow motion reinforced that I didn't imagine what happened.

"Do not cry, for he is with me"

PATRICIA LAMBERT, *Retired Registered Nurse*

In the 1980s, when I was practicing at the National Institutes of Health in Bethesda, Maryland, and also considering joining the LDS Church, I was at the bedside of a patient who was going through the dying process. I had cared for him for several months. After he was pronounced dead, I went into the bathroom to cry, out of the sight of my coworkers and other patients.

As I grieved, I felt a hand on my shoulder and a voice said to me, "Do not cry, for he is with me." The touch was very soft, and I knew there was a presence with me. I felt a warm glow, and a sense of peace came over me. I was shocked.

As I walked out of the bathroom, I felt as if I was floating. A female patient walked up to me and said, "You must have had a spiritual experience. You have a halo around your body." I knew then that the Lord had comforted me. For another patient to see it was affirmation that it did happen.

I was baptized into the LDS Church following this experience, because I knew without a doubt the teachings were true.

"I was really rescued"

JOHAN GOUWS, *Engineer/Investor*

It was 1982 and I was studying engineering in Johannesburg, South Africa, when my car was stolen. A friend of mine was kind and lent me his motorbike to get to campus one day. My classes ended at 5 p.m., forcing me to commute home during peak-hour traffic. To leave the campus I had to cross a very busy road. It took a while, but eventually there was a small gap in the cross traffic and I decided to dash over. But as I pulled away, the motorbike stalled. I jumped off the bike to push it across the street, but I slipped and fell.

When I looked up, I saw a huge bus approaching me very fast. The last thought in my mind was that this bus was going to run me over. At that moment it felt as if someone physically picked me up by the collar and put me, and the motorbike, safely on the other side of the road—albeit with a dislocated shoulder.

My sore shoulder reminds me of that event every day. The experience confirmed my belief in God. I was really rescued. I believe God sent an angel to scoop me up!

"You're really real!"

JOHN BAXTER,
Chief Executive Officer, Consulting Firm

I was confirmed in the local Episcopal church in 1958, when I was fourteen years old. When we came home from church that day, my dad said something like, "Well, congratulations. Now that you're confirmed, you have a choice. You can either go to church each Sunday or you can go sailing with me on Lake Michigan." Needless to say, I chose the sailing and never attended any regular services until 1989.

In 2004, I was facing serious heart surgery with a 5 percent chance of survival. I had never been religious but felt this was one time I needed to pray. A mentor had told me, "Just ask, that's all you have to do." I was very uncomfortable "just asking" and told him I didn't know the proper form to use when praying. He just smiled and said again, "Just ask."

I was sitting on the edge of my hospital bed the day before the surgery and took a deep breath. I then *just asked* God for some help in getting through the operation. All of a sudden a huge weight seemed to lift off my shoulders. I was so much lighter. I felt relaxed and relieved, and I remember looking up at the ceiling and saying, "Wow! I get it. I understand. You're really real!"

I felt amazingly comforted and realized that God had listened and was letting me know that he was going to be there for me even though I hadn't been there for him for years. He didn't say anything; there were no visions—just that five-hundred-pound weight off my shoulders.

I don't tell this story often, but when I do, I well up with tears. The gift of my life has been cherished every day since that moment, and my faith that there is a God will remain with me always.

"I had tried to kill myself"

SHEILA HOWES, *Phlebotomist*

had a fairly normal childhood with loving parents. At eighteen years old I was married and had two children. And then my husband left, and my whole world changed into hell. I started drinking and didn't stop for twenty years.

I ended up having a nervous breakdown and was hospitalized for almost a year. One day I woke up with a thought—"Maybe it's the drink that's causing me so many problems!" It just dawned on me; I hadn't thought of it for twenty years. I rang Alcoholics Anonymous and attended my first meeting.

But after two weeks I was finding it extremely difficult not to drink. I had tried to kill myself before and all I could think about—again—was killing myself.

I woke up one morning and sat at the side of my bed. I felt totally depleted, like an empty shell. I remember saying, "I cannot do this anymore. I cannot go on." I knew I was finished. In the next instant it was as if someone shook me out like a wrinkled sheet. I felt a state of total relaxation, with an enormous feeling of pure love and kindness flowing through my entire body. And then I heard a clear and commanding voice say, "Pray for faith and trust."

At that moment I knew without a doubt that there was a loving power that was looking after me.

My whole outlook on life has changed since this experience because I know I have been given a new life. I have not needed to drink for over nine years now.

"I became aware of a sensation of energy"

FRED MANWARING, *Train Driver*

One day I experienced the most vivid dream. I awoke very distressed because the dream was that my mum was to die in a car accident. Never before had I experienced a dream of such strength, intensity, and realism. I kept the experience private, but I did wonder if it was a premonition. Three years passed, and then Mum died as a result of a car accident.

In the days leading up to the funeral I felt heavy and numb. I requested a private moment with Mum at the funeral home chapel. I approached this visit with angst and deep emotional pain, but I was driven by the need to say a final good-bye.

On reaching the chapel, I walked forward as my wife remained at the entrance. I was filled with profound despair and sadness. A few paces in, I became aware of a sensation of energy at the deepest central point within my body. I stopped walking and drew a deep, hesitant breath. As I did, a flood of warmth started at my feet and moved simultaneously up both legs through my upper body and then dissipated from my head. I became aware of being enveloped in affection and well-being. I could also describe it as great love.

I had no visions, nor did I hear voices, but I became aware of a knowing in my mind that Mum was all right. All my feelings of sadness, pain, and hurt lifted. My emotions changed from overwhelming sadness to a knowing that Mum's existence had not ended, that she was not in pain, and that she was with us. I turned to my wife and said, "Everything is fine. Mum is okay."

I no longer dreaded the following day's service. I remember thinking how beautiful it was. I was smiling inside, at ease, but still very aware of my loss and how my life had changed forever.

From this experience I no longer fear my own death, and I accept the concepts of soul, heaven, and God as true—a belief I did not strongly hold before. I have not been converted to any religion. I still live as I always have done, but I strive to be more accepting of life and family. I try to be more tolerant and to live truthfully—doing what is right without reward, simply because it is right.

It has been fifteen years since Mum's death, and I still have not spoken openly of my experience. I believe that on that day I was blessed with the knowledge of God and a form of afterlife, and how each of us carries a soul that remains linked forever with those we love.

"A violent shock went all through my body"

DR. JON SAINKEN, *Psychiatrist/Investor*

I was twelve and studying for my bar mitzvah. I was reading the Bible and became immersed in religious thinking. It was a period of questioning for me. I questioned God's existence.

One night I had a powerful dream in which I confronted God and challenged him for a sign to prove his existence. Almost immediately there was a tremendous roar and a flash of light, and the mighty hand of God reached out. I felt it might injure or kill me, but only the tip of his forefinger touched me gently on the left temple.

A violent electric shock went all through my body and I woke up badly shaken. I was too terrified to look in the mirror even though my temple was buzzing.

The next morning there was a prominent, uneven scar over my left temple that didn't resemble any usual injury. There was no blood or inflammation, just a scar that looked as though it had always been there. It is still there today.

I learned from this experience to give fair value to what you do understand, and to respect what you don't know.

"I knew I was not alone"

HELEN WOOD, *Retired Clerk*

It was 1998. I was at home with my husband when he said he wasn't feeling well and retired to the bedroom. All of a sudden I heard a half-moan, half-yell come from his direction, and I knew something was terribly wrong. When I reached him, his eyes were rolled back, his tongue was white and sticking out, and he had wet himself. He was dead.

I was terrified and called the emergency number. With their help I was able to perform CPR. As I did, I became very aware that my right arm was feeling different from my left, and I knew I was not alone. It was as if someone else was working my right arm for me.

My husband came back and then died again. I continued CPR and brought him back a second time. The paramedics arrived, got him into the ambulance, and lost him twice on the way to the hospital. But he did end up surviving.

No one will ever convince me I didn't have help from a Higher Power to save his life.

"It was as if a hand turned me completely around"

ANITA CARCONE, *Kindergarten Teacher*

I am an avid competitive swimmer and runner and alternate my swimming and running each day. Early one morning I set out for a run on my usual route near my home on Camelback Road. For the past month there had been construction on the road, and two lanes of traffic had been merged into one. I live on the side of Camelback where the two lanes were merging, so it was especially dangerous to cross the road there.

I was at the end of a thirty-minute run and was nearing home. I had my headset on and was getting into the music when all of a sudden it was as if a hand grabbed me, stopped me, and turned me completely around. I found myself face-to-face with the side of a moving truck. Had I not been pulled around at that exact moment, I would have run right into it.

I must have forgotten about the rerouting of the cars to the other side. I was so shocked by what had happened that my heart raced and I had to catch my breath for several minutes after the incident.

Had that unexplained force, that unseen hand, not turned me around, I would have slammed into that truck and probably would have died. It confirmed to me that I have a special spirit or angel, or somebody who's really watching over me and caring about me. I personally feel I'm here to help the disadvantaged, whether it's a person or an animal. It confirmed to me that I'm here for a reason.

"I felt a tremendous amount
of peace"

TERRY JOHNSON, *Retired Sales Executive*

It was Sunday and the only reason I was going to church was because my son was an altar boy. It was an early mass with only the elderly and us present, and it was boring.

I was at a point in my life where I absolutely hated some people. I knew the hate was wrong and self-defeating and was hurting me. So to diffuse it, every time these people came into my mind, I would tell myself I loved them.

At the end of Mass there was a blessing of the throat. I had had my thyroid removed, so I thought, "Well, I'll go up there and have my throat blessed." As I walked to the front, I felt awkward and embarrassed. I kept wondering where I could look to avoid looking the priest in the eye.

My turn came, and as the priest started to bless my throat, all at once I experienced a tremendous amount of peace. I was enveloped in something. I couldn't see it, but my head, shoulders, and neck felt something I can only describe as love. It felt like God's presence.

As I walked away, I looked around and everything seemed normal. No one else had noticed what had happened to me.

When I picked up my son and told him what had happened, he told me he had experienced the same thing.

I only told my wife and son what had happened to me that day and couldn't even talk about the experience for another five years. To this day I only talk about it when someone is wondering whether God exists.

I think back on the work I was doing at the time to overcome my extreme dislike of some people, and today I wonder if perhaps God was telling me I was doing the right thing by turning my hate into love.

"I want proof that Jesus is real"

MARIE KUTZLI, *Finance Manager*

I was seeking a true God and was reading a book about faith while lying out in the sun. I finished the book and noticed that in the back it said that if you want a relationship with the true and only God, you should say the prayer provided. I thought about it and then said, "Okay God, I'll say this prayer, but I want something to happen. I want proof that Jesus is real." Then I said the prayer.

All of a sudden, from the top of my head to the bottom of my feet, I felt a very slow whitewashing, and I started to speak in an unknown language. I had no clue what it was!

That night I looked in the Yellow Pages to find a church. I picked out a full-gospel Christian church and went. When I walked in, they were all speaking this language. I sat in the back a little freaked out and listened.

The pastor said he'd had a sermon all picked out, but that God had a different plan for the evening, a word for someone. He then said, "You, in the back, in the purple dress." I thought, "There is no way I'm going up there!" So he sent his wife to get me. Reluctantly, I went with her to the front. He then said, "God wants you to know that today your name has been written in the Lamb's Book of Life." I didn't know at that time what the Book of Life was, but I do now, and that day was the first day of my life. On that day my soul was renewed.

At the time this happened, I had been performing Strip-O-Grams for a living. I loved doing it and I made great money. But after this experience, God came into my life and spoke to my heart. It was as if he was saying, "Marie, this job's not for you." My answer back was "You're right!

"I SAW A HUGE, POWERFUL HAND"

Seeing Is Believing

"This, too, shall pass"

LAURA GILMAN, *Special Events Coordinator*

Before my father passed away, he often comforted me by repeating the phrase "This, too, shall pass." It was an expression often said in our house, and it's always had a calming effect on me.

It was 2001. I had just left my job at Morgan Stanley when I went to a party and met and fell for another Morgan Stanley employee—a man named Lindsay Herkness. It was a blissful beginning. We were crazy about each other.

On September 11 we were celebrating the fun six-week period of our relationship. It was my sister's birthday, and Lindsay and I were planning to join my family that night for a special dinner.

At nine o'clock that morning I was in my office on West Fifty-seventh Street reading a *New York Times* article about a former Morgan Stanley colleague who was suing the firm for sexual discrimination. My phone rang just after nine. It was Lindsay.

I remember I was eating cereal out of a plastic cup. I looked down at his business card. It was resting on the base of my Rolodex, on display like a picture. It read: LINDSAY HERKNESS, MORGAN STANLEY, WORLD TRADE TOWER TWO.

"Have you heard?" he asked. "Yes, I'm reading about it," I said, thinking about the news article. "You can't be reading about it—a plane just hit the building. I'm fine. Got to go."

I don't remember what I told him to do. I remember calling

him back and then hanging up because I didn't want him to go back to the phone.

Soon after I got off the phone it became clear to everyone that the city was under attack. Our cell phones didn't work. We were getting word that Washington, D.C., was under attack as well. I was working in the business district and knew it wouldn't be safe to stay there.

I left work and headed home through Central Park. As I arrived home, I felt Lindsay leave the world and I knew he was dead. I was overwhelmed with sadness. I didn't find out the towers had fallen until later that afternoon. I didn't need to know anything else. I knew he was gone and I couldn't even begin to wonder who else from my life went with him.

I cried for two days, alone and with the rest of the city. Had he been the one? I was sure he was. My love and dreams were impossible now, dead. I was inconsolable until a simple sign changed it all.

I was walking to church and passed a streetlight with a sign taped to it. Most of the signs had pictures of missing people on them. This one was different. There were only four words written on this one: THIS, TOO, SHALL PASS.

In a matter of seconds the tears stopped, and I knew my pain would pass, too. At that very moment I knew the Divine was protecting and helping me with words that would mean something powerful to me. I felt guided, protected, and loved.

"The woods lit up as if it was dawn"

LAUREL THOMPSON, Mom

My experience happened before the funeral of one of my best friends. Sue was twenty-four years old and was working as a pilot when she was killed in a plane crash just before Thanksgiving.

I had flown in for the funeral and was staying with Sue's parents along with some other friends. It was probably three o'clock in the morning. I couldn't imagine sleeping and went into a back bedroom to talk with Chris (Sue's husband of less than three months) and Karen (Sue's childhood friend).

When I went into the room, it was so dark I couldn't see anything outside, not even the forest of birch trees I knew was there. We had all been talking for a long time when Chris said, "If there were only some way of knowing that Sue is okay and that she didn't suffer." Within moments, the woods lit up as if it was dawn. I could clearly see the birches in the backyard. It lasted for seconds, and then everything went dark again—as if someone had turned out a light.

We sat there in shock for what seemed like hours until Chris said, "Holy shit, did you guys just see that?" Karen and I nodded and sat there in silence.

The next morning we checked the papers to see if anything unusual had happened weatherwise that night. There was nothing.

"I had a vision of someone looking at me from above"

MINTER KROTZER, *Writer*

In midtown Manhattan, on Lexington Avenue and Fifty-fourth Street, is a very small white chapel. It's nestled within St. Peter's Lutheran Church at the foot of the Citicorp Building, one of the tallest buildings in the city.

About ten years ago, when I was working in this neighborhood, I went to this chapel all the time. I went during lunch, coffee breaks, and after work. At first I went because I needed a break from my life: I had a stressful job as a paralegal at one of the largest law firms in the city, my boyfriend was an alcoholic, and I suffered from depression and anxiety. I found I needed to be there, to experience the silence, and to be still. It calmed me down like nothing else could.

The chapel is entirely white, with painted white floors, and is named after the artist Louise Nevelson, who designed the interior. She made the sculptures along the walls and the crucifix above the altar. They are simple structures, made of wood, abstract and not figurative. I'd often sit in a pew and gaze at them, noticing the shadows of people walking by through the fogged glass window. Then I'd close my eyes and experience the silence, with only the distant sounds of midtown in the background. I'd sit for a long time, sometimes for my whole lunch hour.

Then one day while I was sitting there, I realized I was praying. I immediately convinced myself I wasn't. "I am not praying.

I am thinking," I said to myself over and over. I had no intention of being someone who prayed—not one of *those* people.

After this experience I took a break from going to the chapel
for a while. I didn't want to find myself praying again, but then,
on a day that was particularly bad at work, I went back. I allowed myself to sink into the silence, to be enveloped by it. I
didn't care what happened: I needed the peace. And then, as I
sat there, I had a vision of someone looking at me from above,
outside of the chapel and beyond, from another realm. I was
being observed, but I couldn't see the observer, and I witnessed
this as if I were outside my physical body. There was a sense of
concern and propriety about the observer, and I felt greatness. I
realized I was being observed by God.

In that next year I started going to church again and came to
believe in God in a way I never had before. I began to pray reg-
ularly and without shame. Over the years, my life changed.

I see now that I came to God through the silence. I began
by craving silence—not God—but it is in the silence that I
found God.

"I saw a huge, powerful hand"

GREGORY WORTHLEY,
Telecommunications Sales Representative

I was not raised in a religious family. I always believed in God but never felt his presence in my life. I never felt that God was "there."

In 2000 I went through a divorce. Afterward, I was very lonely and became an alcoholic. I was struggling financially and was on the verge of bankruptcy. Basically, I was en route to hitting rock bottom. My entire life was in a downward spiral.

One day it occurred to me that I needed to do something about it, so I decided to go to a local church. That day I went to church and prayed to God to come into my life.

That afternoon I fell into my normal Sunday routine of watching football and relaxing, but that night my life changed.

I was lying asleep facedown when I was awakened by a deep, strong voice that said my name. I felt as if I was in a state—somewhere between being asleep and awake. I thought, "I just heard someone say my name, but it's just me and my two dogs in the bedroom." I tried to turn over and, as I did, I felt a hurricane-force wind blowing so strongly at my back that I was prevented from moving. I literally felt my skin flapping.

I looked behind me, and out of the corner of my eye I saw a huge, powerful hand extending from clouds with bolts of lightning reaching out to me. And then the voice said, "You asked me to come into your life." At that moment I knew something crazy was going on and that God was in my room talking to me.

I responded, "How will I know you are there?" and his voice answered, "Worship me and you will know." And then everything stopped.

I became more alert and aware and found myself in a cold sweat. I sat up in bed, terribly frightened about what had just happened.

When I settled back into bed, I decided to lie faceup because I wanted to see God if he came again. I was still frightened. But as I lay there, I began to think about what had happened. As I drifted off to sleep, I felt an incredible, peaceful, tingling feeling going through my entire body.

The next day I woke up a changed person. I am back on my feet financially, have grown substantially as a Christian, and have overcome my alcohol addiction (though it is still something I struggle with all the time). I really feel blessed and will never forget this experience. Even though God's message was very simple, it was profound and true.

"My wife threatened divorce
if I continued"

ROBERT ABRAHAMS, *Artist*

At the age of forty-five I began to question. I wondered if there was a meaning to my life. I always believed that God existed, but I didn't know why I believed and I didn't know what I was supposed to do with this knowledge.

I began a long, academic search that eventually led me to Sufism, the spiritual core of Islam. I decided I should become a Muslim.

I made this decision during the First Gulf War and, as you can imagine, my plans elicited a strong reaction from my Christian family. My wife threatened divorce if I continued. I was distraught, not wishing my spiritual journey to end in a divorce.

While I was in this state of turmoil, I awoke one night to see a figure standing at the foot of my bed. I was very fearful, thinking it was an intruder. The figure was dressed in deep green robes and was wearing a turban. I received a nonverbal communication—to keep searching and all would become clear. And then the figure disappeared.

I awoke the next morning feeling very different, and my life has not been the same since. My wife complains that I'm not the man she married (which I take as a compliment). I eventually became a member of the Baha'i Faith, a faith that stems from Islam the way Christianity comes from Judaism. We understand that religion is progressive and that all the prophets come with the same spiritual concepts. We don't see conflict between

HPL Central
Renewals by Phone 832-393-2280

Customer ID: **********891

Title: God stories : inspiring encounters with the
divine / edited by Jennifer Skiff.
ID: 33477458608364
Due: 08-14-10

Total items: 1
7/31/2010 2:37 PM

HPL Central

religions. The aim is to resolve problems of the world through spiritual means.

I am now seventy-six years old and am very active as an artist and am also involved in community service. That experience confirmed for me the existence of God and led me to my current state, in which I still have a wife—and my spirituality.

"I started falling asleep at the wheel"

BEVERLY STOCKI, *Dental Hygienist*

I was twenty-three years old when I had my encounter with the Divine. My husband and I lived in Erie, Pennsylvania, and were setting off on a ten- to twelve-hour drive to New York City for a wedding. We first drove three hours to my mom's in Pittsburgh and had a short visit, then took off again from there at 1 a.m.

I told my husband I would drive since he had worked all day. I had been driving for six hours and was still on the turnpike when, at about 7 a.m., I started falling asleep at the wheel. I remember my body being extremely cozy in the seat of the car as I laid my head against the window.

I have no idea what woke me up. But as I opened my eyes, God was kneeling on the hood of my car, directly in front of me, with his hands in the praying position at his chest. He was a full-blown person and the wind wasn't moving his hair or the robe he was wearing. His head was bowed, but his eyes were looking right into mine.

I immediately pulled off to the side of the road and he disappeared. My husband woke up and said, "What's wrong?" I slumped back into my seat, still staring out the window and said, "You drive. I just saw God!"

Believe me, I am not a religious fanatic. I don't see visions. But this happened to me. That was in 1967, and to this day I feel so very blessed for having had the opportunity to see him in person.

"I could not take my son with me"

MICHELE CERAMI, *Investment Adviser*

It was 1989. I was two years into a postpartum depression after the birth of my only son. I was gritting it out, doing yoga, meditation, and nature walks and reading every spiritual book I could get my hands on. I was determined to get better without drugs.

Some days were better than others. My boyfriend and I had just broken up, and I had taken two steps backward in my healing and was feeling extremely depressed. My two-year-old son was taking a nap and I decided to have a bath, something I liked doing when I felt bad.

I was sitting toward the front of the tub, staring at nothing but saying to myself over and over that I didn't want to live if this was what life was like. It was too hard. Not that I wanted to end my life—I just couldn't go on feeling the way I was feeling. I felt as if I wanted to die and yet I didn't.

All of a sudden, to the left of me in my peripheral vision, a scene appeared as though a portal had opened up and I was able to see this "place." I never had to turn my head—I could just see it clearly, although it was to the side of me. I saw a stream about ten feet wide and three feet deep. I could see everything as if I was standing on the right-hand side of the stream. On the other side was just white light, and I thought of it as the "land of light." There was no voice, but the message conveyed to me was to "cross the stream to the other side where the light is and there will be no more pain." I would be peaceful. It felt like a loving invitation. I stood there on my side and thought how tempting the invitation was—no more pain.

I looked around from where I was standing, and although I was alone in a country-type setting, I could see the rest of the world and humanity in the distance, as if I were standing apart from them. I thought that if I crossed over the stream into the "land of light," I would not feel all my feelings like I had on earth—in other words, I wouldn't feel my humanity. I was torn as to whether I should cross, because my humanity at this point was pretty painful and yet I wasn't sure I was willing to give up the pain! Then, at that instant, I realized I could not take my son with me.

The moment that thought came into my mind, I knew I would not cross and the whole vision disappeared.

I have always questioned the existence of a "God"—relentlessly, actually. I've had several experiences now. Do I believe in God, though? The only thing I know for sure from all my experiences is that they are filled with love, peace, and the unity of all things that is unlike anything I have ever felt in my normal state of consciousness.

"Miracles do happen"

Natural Medicine Practitioner

I n 1996 I was diagnosed with a massive brain tumor that one neurosurgeon described as being a "monster." It was the size of an orange. At first, doctors didn't think they would be able to get it out and told me that if they couldn't, I would have three months to live. Eventually they decided they would try to get it by going through my ear.

From the day the doctors gave me my diagnosis up until my surgery, I became totally focused on healing. I put my trust in God that the tumor would come out easily and that there wouldn't be any side effects of paralysis, blindness, or death (to name a few). I wrote and spoke affirmations to God all day, every day, day and night. I filled my bedroom with paintings and affirmations. I bought a sticker that said MIRACLES DO HAPPEN and stuck it above my bed on the wall with blue tack.

A week after sticking the MIRACLES DO HAPPEN sticker on the wall, I was getting ready for bed and noticed it was lying faceup on my pillow. I didn't think anything of it, and I stuck it back up. The next night I went to bed and there it was again on my pillow faceup. I thought I mustn't have stuck it firmly enough, so back it went, nice and firm. Again, the next night I went to bed and, yes, there it was—MIRACLES DO HAPPEN was on my pillow. This time I went around the house and asked my husband, children, parents, and friends, "Who has been in my bedroom and touched my sticker?" Everyone said they hadn't. I went back into my room and looked at the pillow, and all of a sudden it hit me. God had put it there! I burst into tears and thanked God and my angels. "Yes," I said, "miracles do happen, and that's what's going to happen to me." I got it! I put the sticker back on the wall and it never fell off again.

When I went into the hospital, I took it with me and stuck it on my hospital bed. The operation lasted seventeen hours, and in the end, the doctors couldn't get it all.

It wasn't until a week after being in intensive care that I noticed my sticker was gone from my bed. I smiled and was full of love as I realized I didn't need it anymore. The miracle had happened.

Five years later, the portion of the tumor the doctors were unable to get the first time had grown. It was inoperable because of its location. I had a procedure called stereotactic radiosurgery, a type of radiation. That was six years ago. Today I feel God has healed me.

I believe these things happen to teach you things about yourself. I didn't get the message the first time, so he needed to touch me a second time. I'm not the same person I was ten years ago. My heart is open to myself and everyone else. What a gift I've been given! Every day is a gift.

"His love and compassion hit my heart"

CHRIS RAE, *Internet Network Designer*

I was brought up in a Christian home and went to a large Pente-costal church throughout my childhood. When I was nine-teen, I realized I didn't have the relationship with God I thought I had. I left the church and went my own way.

Nine years later I was hurting. My parents had broken up and my family was a mess. I was living each day to get by and didn't know if there was a point in living at all. I was walking around feeling constantly rejected and in pain. I was angry at the church that was supposed to lead me closer to God. I wasn't going to believe God was there just because other people said he was. I had never seen him or heard him speak. So as far as I was concerned, when you died, there was nothing.

Most of my friends were Christian, and together we were doing a course on communing with God. I disagreed with it, and because I knew Scripture well, I was able to shake their faith. But despite my behavior and the fact that I held these views, I was still open, and I remember standing in my apartment saying, "God or the Higher Power, whoever made me, if you're real I would like to know."

A few months later, a friend's mum, Theresa, started a church at her home and I went along. I stayed after everyone left and decided to talk to Theresa about my life and family problems. I was getting very emotional when she said, "Do you mind if I ask Jesus to be a part of this conversation?" I replied sarcastically, "If you want—whatever that means."

We began to discuss something that had happened to me as a child. I told her about a teacher I'd had who had been very abusive. She caned me for things I didn't do. And she wouldn't let me go to the bathroom. When I inevitably wet myself, she told my parents I was a troublemaker.

Theresa asked me to close my eyes and visualize the classroom. I did. Then she asked me to describe the room. I was doing that when she said, "Look around. Do you see Jesus anywhere?" I looked around the room. Yes! He was there. He was glowing with a radiant light. It wasn't a normal light—it was a living light, and his love and compassion hit my heart. It felt like the first time I had ever felt love in my heart. At that moment, he took the pain away.

I've never questioned since.

"My pain disappeared"

NEIL WOLLPERT, *Insurance Sales Representative*

I was suffering from unremitting pain throughout my body twenty-four hours a day. My journey to get a diagnosis and some relief took me to hospitals at Ohio State University, the Indiana University School of Medicine, the Mayo Clinic, Harvard Medical School, and the Cleveland Clinic. The Cleveland Clinic was the last hospital out of the five I went to. I had seen twenty medical specialists, and still no one could help me. I was miserable and I considered suicide because there was not a moment during this whole time that I wasn't in pain.

Then, at three o'clock one morning, I was awakened by a golden light in the upper corner of our bedroom. It was an odd light, about a foot and a half around in diameter. It was dense in the middle and got thinner on the outside. And then I heard a voice inside my head say, "Everything will be all right." At the exact moment I heard the voice, I knew it was real, because my pain disappeared. For the first time in five and a half years, I didn't have pain. Five minutes passed and the light slowly faded, and as it did, my pain returned.

At first I thought I had imagined the whole thing, but to be pain-free for just those five minutes was proof to me that God had touched me personally. It was a *Wow!* kind of thing.

I have now been diagnosed with fibromyalgia and am on medication for the pain. Since my experience with the golden light, my faith has waned, and I remain a constant seeker, but I do not question God's existence.

"Words that tasted like honey"

SEBIO AGUILAR, *Retired Machine Operator*

It was April 23, 1983. I remember it as if it were yesterday. I was at an evening service at the Latin American Assembly of God church in Hanford, California, when the pastor asked those who wanted to, to come forward and pray at the altar. Some senior members of the church waited at the front to assist those coming forward in prayer. It just happened that when I went up, my brother and sister-in-law stood beside me.

I knelt and prayed. As I prayed, the words had a taste to them that made me not want to stop. I remember praying for about fifteen minutes when I heard my sister-in-law say, "You are receiving the Holy Spirit." I continued praying. I didn't want to quit. Each word had a honey taste to it. I didn't know what I was saying—it was just words that tasted like honey.

As I continued, I had a vision. I saw myself in a barren land. Before me was a wall. I walked to the wall and climbed it, and then climbed some stairs until I reached two huge doors. They were so big I felt like a tiny ant looking up. I banged on one of the doors and it opened slightly. I slipped inside and all I could hear was singing. It sounded like thousands of people singing, but I couldn't see them. It was mind-boggling. It was a sound I had never heard before. It was so beautiful.

Around me was crystal rock everywhere. I had never seen this rock before. I couldn't identify it. It was absolutely beautiful. As I walked, I saw a figure coming toward me. I could hear people singing praises to the Lord. I didn't see a face, but I could sense it was a man. He was wearing a robe with a silver-and-white collar. I fell to my knees and bowed. I saw the sandals and the punctures on his feet. When he extended his arms down, I saw the punctures on his palms, and I knew it was Jesus himself.

The only words he said were "Welcome, my son." At that moment I felt a hand on my shoulder, and as I turned around, I realized it was my sister-in-law. My brother was sitting in the front pew of the church and everyone else was gone. I asked how long I had been there, and she said, "Four hours!" It was 11:45 p.m. I had stepped up to the altar at 7 p.m. "You were speaking a different language!" my sister-in-law said. "You were with the Holy Spirit, and we didn't know what you were saying."

I've had dreams and nightmares all my life, but I can't recall them. I remember this vision as if it were an actual trip I went on. To this day I can tell you everything about it. It remains with me and is extremely vivid. Everything I had learned as a child but never understood became clear to me during those four hours of prayer.

"I KNEW WHEN SHE PASSED AWAY"

Confirming the Afterlife

"I felt love, joy, and happiness all in one big bubble"

ALLAN HEFFERNAN, *Retired Engineering Technician*

On November 18, 1991, our family lost a beautiful boy, my son Steve, to suicide. He was twenty years old and had suffered years of turmoil.

The week before the funeral, we were home as a family, going through recurring bouts of grief and crying. I was pacing back and forth in our living room. For some reason a thought came to me, and I blurted out, "I never got a hug good-bye!"

The week progressed and we had the burial. A day later, I went upstairs to bed feeling very tired and settled into a good sleep. Sometime before morning, I got up, sat on the edge of the bed, stood up, and proceeded to go downstairs. Everything was quiet in the house as I walked into the living room. As I entered the dining room, I saw a human figure in front of me. The person, whose face I couldn't see, was holding his hands high over has his head and I realized that he wanted a hug. So I put my arms around the person and gave him a hug. And I felt him hug me back. The feelings I had at the moment were almost indescribable. I felt bubbly, like a cork floating in a champagne bottle. I felt love, joy, and happiness all in one big bubble.

The next thing I remember was sitting up in bed filled with great joy and saying, "That was my son!"

Some people may say I was dreaming. But for me, it was an out-of-body experience in which I connected with my son. I know what happened. I know it was real, and no one can tell me differently.

At the moment I was hugged, I knew we would never, ever be separated and he was in a safe place and still so much alive. I am so grateful this was allowed to happen to me. All my life I have been a believer, but this experience was my first recognition that everything I believed was true.

"It was the mailman delivering a surprise package"

LAWRENCE GROFF, *Retired Attorney*

On March 6, 1967, my sister Patricia was stabbed to death in her bedroom on the island of Java in Bandung, Indonesia.

Pat had been in Indonesia for two months and was working as a teacher for the children of missionaries. It had been her goal since she was twelve to do this work. She was twenty-five years old.

Her murderer was a nineteen-year-old who said he broke into her apartment to rob a wealthy American. But there was nothing to rob. She had been living out of a suitcase, still waiting for her clothing and personal items to arrive by ship.

I was working in New York when I received the call from my father telling me of this horrible event. I immediately returned to be with my parents in Pawtucket, Rhode Island.

Two days later we learned that Pat's body would arrive in the United States on Thursday, March 9. On the ninth I called KLM Airlines to check on the plane's estimated time of arrival at Kennedy International Airport. I was told it would be 3 p.m., fifteen minutes earlier than originally scheduled. At exactly 3 p.m., as the plane carrying Pat touched down at Kennedy, the doorbell rang at our home. It was the mailman delivering a surprise package with Pat's handwriting on it. In it were gifts she had purchased and mailed for friends and family when she stopped in Singapore on her way to her missionary job in Indonesia. It was an eerie feeling. I felt that a force had caused this to happen and that Pat's surprise was actually herself, coming home.

I believe God has a way of letting us know of his existence by sending messages as he did on that day. God might have done this to make us aware that Pat would remain a part of our lives forever. Or, the message might be that we are to give gifts of love and forgiveness to one another and try to live the loving life that Pat did.

Pat read the Bible before going to sleep each night. The night she was murdered, it was open to John 12:24 (New Living Translation): "The truth is, a kernel of wheat must be planted in the soil. Unless it dies it will be alone—a single seed. But its death will produce many new kernels—a plentiful harvest of new lives."

"On her way to heaven"

MARTY CROAK, *Attorney*

Cindy and I met at the post office where we both worked. She was a beautiful woman—full of energy with a great smile. We fell in love.

It wasn't long before she was complaining of stomach pains and was diagnosed with colon cancer. At nineteen years old, she had part of her colon removed and went through chemotherapy. Soon she was feeling better and we resumed a normal life. We got engaged and bought a house, and I started law school.

But the pain started again. Doctors opened her up. The cancer had spread. We were told she was terminal. I decided not to continue with law school that semester. Instead, I worked at the post office and went to Cindy after work. She was moved from the hospital to a bed in her parents' living room, and every night that's where I visited her.

One morning I was startled awake in the bedroom of the house we had bought together. I felt a jolt in my heart, as if something was going through it. And then an incredible sense of peace came over me. I looked out the window and saw a beautiful sunrise. A few minutes later the phone rang. It was Cindy's father. Cindy had just died.

After hanging up, I knew I had been awakened by Cindy's soul passing through me on her way to heaven.

"I knew when she passed away"

MIKE MORGAN, *Insurance Agency Owner*

Near the end of my mother's ten-year battle with cancer, my brother and sister and I rotated days taking care of her. On my day I would lift her from the bed to the wheelchair, laugh with her, and cry with her. I did this for two months.

On the night she passed away, my brother, Dana, was with her. I was sleeping in my home two hours away. I awoke to the sound of my name being called: "Mike!" And then I felt shock waves, like electric shocks going from my head to my feet. It was an amazing feeling. I looked at the clock and it was 3:45 a.m. The phone rang at 5:50. It was Dana saying Mom was gone. He had checked on her at 3:00 and she was breathing, but at 4:00, she wasn't. He didn't know when she had passed.

I told him I knew exactly when she passed away. The experience left me with an inner peace I still have to this day.

My wife has always dragged me to church for Christmas and Easter, but it wasn't until this experience with my mom that I knew. I feel I received a gift at that moment that showed me we are all connected and that we don't die but instead graduate to something greater.

"I'll Take You Home Again, Kathleen"

KATHLEEN RHOADS,
Customer Service Representative

My dad had always been a very happy-go-lucky guy. He loved life and always had a good time. He was a musician and a great singer. All the parties were at our house! I was his firstborn, and my parents named me Kathleen. So for any and practically every event, my father would sing to me the song "I'll Take You Home Again, Kathleen."

Twenty years had passed since Dad was taken by God—quite suddenly, to everyone's shock. I never got to say good-bye, and it had always bothered me. Over the years I had moments of sadness, but on one particular night in 2002, I was overwhelmed by it.

I was working behind the bar in the Delta Crown Room and was overcome with sadness, missing my dad. I became very melancholy and just couldn't keep it together. I was about to tell the guy I was working with that I was going to go home early when the elevator door opened and a man who looked like my dad came walking toward me. It was really spooky. Dad always wore a suit, tie, and hat. This man was dressed the same way and even had a similar stature.

He walked straight up to me and said, "Is your name Kathleen?" (I wasn't wearing a name tag that night). I told him it was. And then he started singing "I'll Take You Home Again, Kathleen"! I just stood there, stunned. He sang all the verses and then turned around and walked out. He didn't even have a drink. That wasn't like my dad—he would've had a drink.

My coworkers asked me who he was. I told them I had never seen him before. And I have never seen him since.

Since then I have been at peace with my father's passing. I think that God gives us lots of little clues. He knows what's going on. When he sees us in pain, he helps us. I believe God sent this man to help me through my sadness.

"The birds started singing"

MICHELE CROAN, *Shop Owner*

My mom passed away on July 3, 2006. We were extremely close—like sisters. During the next week I would catch a whiff of her perfume or the soap she used. It made me feel good. Everyone was worried about me and how I was, but I had an amazing feeling of faith, like none I had ever experienced. But it was the day after the funeral when I experienced the most up-lifting feeling.

It was Sunday morning, and I went out on the deck to have coffee with my husband. We were sitting about ten feet from a tree and a bird feeder. Usually at this time of the morning, the feeders were loaded with birds, but on this morning there were only two birds, a mother and her chick.

I guessed that it must have been the baby bird's first time out of the nest by the way it was wanting to be fed. I sat and watched this wonderful act of nature while the mother bird taught the baby to feed on its own. My husband and I sat in silence for forty-five minutes and watched. I felt I was in a trance. I remember looking at the mother bird and her baby and associating them with my mother and myself.

That afternoon, when I was alone, I stepped outside, and the two birds were there again. This time the baby made its way to the feeder, fed itself, and flew to the birdbath. The mother flew off into the woods, and the little bird sat for some time by itself. I felt alone, like the little bird. But I also felt that my mom was sending me a message: "It's okay. You're on your own." As much as I felt comforted, I sat down and cried—a good cry. And as I sat there crying, the birds started singing in the nearby trees. Then they all joined the baby on the feeder.

It was reassuring for me. It was God's way of telling me that everything is okay, and everything is going to *be* okay.

"I'll be right there, Pop"

KATHLEEN MACDONALD,
Pharmacy Supervisor

A few days a week I would go to my aunt's home to care for my ailing ninety-three-year-old grandfather. On one particular day I was running a few minutes late, so I wasn't surprised to hear my grandfather call my name as I walked through the doorway. I yelled up to his room, "I'll be right there, Pop." At the same time, my cousin's wife yelled from the kitchen, "She's not here yet, Pop," not knowing I had just walked in.

I went up to my grandfather's room to say good morning but found he had passed away. It was obvious he had been dead for some time because he was cold to the touch and the blood had settled to one side of his body. As I ran down the steps, I yelled for my cousin to call 911. I told her Pop was dead. She said, "He can't be dead, he just called your name!"

When the police and rescue team got there, I asked how long they thought he had been dead. It was their assumption he had been gone at least three hours before I got there.

I had already had a strong belief in God before this happened, but this experience confirmed it.

"I saw the most beautiful shooting star"

MARTHA THOMPSON,
University Principal Secretary

On the day before Thanksgiving in 2006, a very special friend of mine named Larry passed away. That night I did what I do every night at ten o'clock—I took my two dogs for a walk and talked to God. On this night I also asked Larry to let me know he had made it to heaven by showing me a beautiful shooting star. But I didn't see one.

The next night I took the dogs for a walk and made the same request, but again no shooting star.

I didn't tell anyone what I had asked for. It was just between God, Larry, the dogs, and me.

The next night was the funeral. I went with my husband, and my daughter agreed to meet us there. When she arrived, she walked straight up to me and said, "Mom, I just saw the most beautiful shooting star on my way over here."

My heart overflowed. I cried because it confirmed everything. God was letting me know Larry was in heaven.

"Morning Has Broken"

RITA WHITEMAN, *Homemaker*

On May 7, 2003, I crawled into bed with my mother and sang her the song "Morning Has Broken," hoping she would let go. It was the last morning of her life. Since her passing I've had a quirky thing about time. If I happen to glance at the clock and it's 10:10, 11:11, 12:12, and so forth, I'll look heavenward and say, "Hi, Mom." It seems to happen more often than coincidentally, more than happenstance.

On October 31, 2006, my mother's birthday, my brother was near death. I was working at home that day, listening to the radio, and "Morning Has Broken" came on. I looked at the clock and the time was 1:11. And then it was almost as if I heard my mother's voice. I felt my mother near me saying, "Don't worry. I'll be here to meet him."

My brother passed away peacefully at about eight o'clock that evening. I have no doubt she was there to greet him.

I don't care what religion you are. I think there's a God that looks over all of us. I believe we live on in many ways, shapes, and forms.

"How Great Thou Art"

PATI FREY, *Retired Sales Manager Executive*

My mother-in-law, Ann, was turning eighty and, unbeknownst to her, everyone flew to her winter residence in Naples, Florida, for a surprise birthday party. She was thrilled. Her children were there along with her brother and sisters. It was a wonderful day.

Within weeks, though, she was dying from complications of an infection in her spine. She flew home to Pennsylvania for medical attention, and we began an around-the-clock vigil at her bedside. One evening, exhausted from prayer, I suggested we sing. So about eight of us surrounded her and sang her favorite song, "How Great Thou Art." She died the next morning.

The day of the funeral, I was asked to drive her car to the service. I had my two children with me. It was a solemn time, and the radio was off. I wanted it quiet.

As we were pulling up to the church, the radio came on all by itself, playing "How Great Thou Art." It was just that song—there was no song before it. My children saw it—I did not touch the radio. And there was no way you could turn on the radio from the steering wheel.

It confirmed to me that God was there. I never thought I would observe his grace firsthand. I haven't needed further convincing. It also made me feel that Ann was saying, "It's okay. I'm okay. Everyone will be okay."

"Donald has sent us a sign!"

JULIA BONADONNA DZIEWISZ,
College Professor

During my brother Donald's last week he could not speak, but we knew he could hear us. There were ten family members with him at his home when he passed. Exactly two hours later, there was an incredible, unexplainable rainbow over the house. It was overcast and it wasn't raining. I saw it and said, "Look, Donald has sent us a sign!" I then told my family that before Donald passed away, I had whispered in his ear that I wanted him to send me a sign when he got to the other side, to let me know he was all right and in heaven. My sisters both remarked that they had also asked him for a sign.

We called my sister-in-law to come and see the rainbow. We told her that we had asked for a sign. What we didn't know is that she had also asked for a sign. She had asked Donald to send her a rainbow!

At first I thought, "This is a wonderful sign, but is it really my brother?" Maybe it was just a coincidence. Then I thought of my parents—heartbroken after losing their only son—and my seven-year-old nephew, who had just lost his father. I wanted them to believe Donald had sent the rainbow. That was the most important thing. But for myself, I needed more confirmation.

I think my brother sensed my skepticism, because every time I began to think it was a coincidence, another rainbow appeared on a significant date. On the one-year anniversary of my brother's death, a double rainbow appeared over the top of his wife and son's house. I have a picture of it. My belief in God was confirmed by that first rainbow and has been strengthened by all the rainbows I've seen since.

"It was total sorrow and sadness"

TERESA PARADIS,
Executive Director, Live and Let Live Farm Rescue

A s a young girl I had a dream to work for an animal rescue organization that saved horses. In 1996 I formed Live and Let Live Farm Rescue. The farm is an animal shelter that rescues horses and other animals in danger of starvation, abuse, neglect, or abandonment.

In March 2004 I received a call from one of our board members asking for help. Nancy said a friend of hers, Harry, was very sick and was concerned about his horses. She told me that Harry loved his three horses more than anything in the world, but a family member was considering putting the horses to rest once Harry had passed. Harry's wife was hoping I could save them.

I agreed to meet with Harry and his wife, Hope, at 1 p.m. but decided to see the horses first. Nancy came with me. When we arrived, they were standing in a back pasture and were very happy. They followed us around and let us scratch their necks, rub them all over, and breathe in their noses. As we left, the horses followed us back through the barn and up to the edge of the fence.

As I turned to get into the car, I looked back. The demeanor of the horses had completely changed. Their heads were down; their bodies were slumped. They looked as if they were crying. I was overwhelmed. I had never felt such sadness in my entire life—it was total sorrow and sadness. I looked at Nancy and said, "Oh my God, Nancy, those horses are so sad. They must really be missing Harry."

We then went to meet with Harry. He was staying five minutes away. When we arrived, Hope answered the door and said, "Harry's just passed. I've just called the priest." The hair stood up all over me as I realized what had just happened.

The moment I had seen the sadness in those horses, they must have known what was happening. Harry was passing over at that very moment and saying his good-bye. I now feel strongly that Harry would not pass away until he knew his horses would be safe. Just moments before I saw the sadness in the horses, I had decided to take all three of them to the shelter.

The spirits of our loved animals are strongly connected to us. Harry loved his horses. If I wasn't a believer before, I was a believer right then and there.

"He passed right through me"

MARK MCENTEE, *Composer*

Michael Hutchence was a pretty good friend of mine. He was a gentle person with a lovely spirit. We were both Australian musicians and had that in common, but we also had the same interest in culture. He was a very cultured person.

When we had the time, we'd hang out. Sometimes that was in Sydney, where we both worked out of the same recording studio. Other times it was in America, when he was touring with INXS and I was touring with the Divinyls.

Michael died on November 22, 1997. A few months after the funeral, I was working in a recording studio in Sydney. I had finished the instrumental recording and was doing the vocal tracks. As I was standing in the back of the room listening to the playback, I felt Michael's spirit pass right through me. The feeling I got was the actual vibrancy of his spirit. It was a beautiful energy—his energy. And then, from my heart, I heard him say, "I am in a beautiful place."

The experience lasted about ten seconds. Afterward I looked around at the other people in the room and said, "Wow! Michael Hutchence just came to me!"

It was a very vivid, true feeling. Nothing like that had ever happened to me before.

It was a real afterlife experience. It confirmed for me that the essence of Michael's soul—his youth and vibrancy—was in a good place and that indeed there is something after the death experience.

"I don't believe in coincidence"

EARL BRECHLIN, *Journalist*

I don't believe in coincidence. We are all guilty of shrugging off as coincidence moments of cosmic clarity or focus. Most of the time we aren't even aware they've happened. Often we are too busy, working too hard, or just simply oblivious to the interconnectedness of the events around us. When we do experience a glimmer of recognition, when some emotional button deep within our souls is pushed, we often dismiss it as déjà vu. Few people have the time or inclination to dwell on exactly what it was that sparked those feelings, to trace it back, peel off the layers, reveal the roots. These bits and pieces, and the memories we associate with them, will bubble to the surface unpredictably. Who knows what triggers them—a fleeting thought, a familiar pattern of light, a sound, a scent, or the gentle brush of a summer breeze. And then there are other times when a clear sign, an unmistakable message, just walks right up and hits you over the head.

It happened to me in July 2002. I was driving to my home in Bar Harbor, Maine, from a bookstore where I had been promoting my postcard book *Bygone Bar Harbor*. I was thinking about my upcoming wedding and wishing some of my dear departed relatives were with me to share it.

I began thinking about my grandmother Barbara Brechlin (Baba). I was named after her husband, Earl, who died just before I was born. I never knew my grandfather, but I carried his memory, not only as his namesake but also in my stewardship of a treasured symbol of his love.

Not long before Baba died, she gave me the diamond engagement ring her Earl had given to her in 1929 in Meriden, Connecticut. I understood it was not easy for her to give away something that she had carried so close to her heart for more than fifty years. She said she wanted me to have it so I could give it to the woman I would marry. I kept it safely stored away for fifteen years, until I proposed to Roxie.

When I got home from the bookstore, I began searching through the thousands of postcards I had of Mount Desert Island and Acadia National Park, Maine, for one a friend had asked for.

The cards were stored in plastic sleeves, two cards back-to-back, front side out. In all the binders I looked through, there was just one slot where a single card was missing. Even though I seldom pay any attention to the address side of the postcards, my gaze stalled on the back of one. I stared, not comprehending what I saw. It was a postcard from Bar Harbor, Maine, addressed to Mrs. Earl Brechlin, Colony Street, Meriden, Connecticut. It was postmarked July 1956.

Until that moment, I was unaware I possessed a card that Baba had once held in her hand—a postcard delivered to the house where I had lived some forty-six years before, sent from a place I would eventually call home. And then there was the date on the card. It was written on July 11. My first date with my fiancée, Roxie, in Bar Harbor, was on July 11.

So just how did a postcard sent from Bar Harbor, written to my grandmother on a particular day forty-six years before, just happen to end up in the hands of a Massachusetts dealer who just happened to sell it to me at an antiques show in Connecticut? And how did I just happen to not discover it was in my possession until two years later, just minutes after thinking about the woman who gave away her most precious possession to be worn by my bride just a few days later?

Could that all really be just a coincidence? I wouldn't bet on it. Here was something much more powerful than a simple piece of old paper. Here was a spiritual echo, an emotional ripple, a sign, postmarked from Maine for delivery far in the future, a message, seemingly lost yet destined to be found, in an amazing cosmic collision of life and love and time.

"I HAVE SOMETHING TO TELL YOU"

Getting That Feeling

"It was clearly God"

STEPHEN SMITH,
Retired Superintendent of Heating, Ventilation,
and Air-Conditioning Construction

I t was 1972. I had been married for four years and things weren't going great between my wife and me. We had two children: our daughter was three years old and our son was almost one.

I was working in Chicago on a downtown high-rise as a sheet metal worker. One day my wife dropped me off at work. She didn't bring me lunch that day and didn't pick me up after work. When I got home, I realized she had packed up and left. She was gone, and she had taken the kids.

I assumed she had gone to her father's house in Georgia, but I didn't know how to reach him. I checked with friends and family. She hadn't told anyone what she was doing. No one knew where they were.

I figured I'd hear from her sooner or later, but I kept searching. Six weeks passed and nothing. I was becoming more and more concerned about the kids, and I was missing them. As time passed, a thought kept growing, building in the back of my mind. I kept thinking, "They're somewhere here." I looked everywhere. I talked to everyone. Still, this same thought kept going through my mind. And then I had an impulse to check out a babysitter we had used once or twice more than a year before. I hadn't liked her. I didn't think she was responsible, and she hadn't kept a clean house. But I couldn't remember where she lived. And then I thought it didn't make sense to check with this woman, because she had babysat for us before my son was even born.

But the impulse got stronger, and I started thinking about the area where she had lived. I was still working, but now I was consumed with this thought. One Friday after work the impulse was so strong I couldn't think of much else. I remember sitting back into a meditative state to concentrate on this thought. And then I remembered where she lived! I got in my car and drove to the house.

A child opened the door, and as I stepped in, my daughter came running up to me. I looked over to where my son was. He was in a playpen and was standing up, holding onto those little bars, and as he saw me, he lifted up his little arms and started crying.

The woman told me my wife had dropped them off with two weeks' worth of babysitting money, but that she had never come for them or been in touch again. She said she didn't know how to get hold of me. She had had the children for six weeks. This was on a Friday. She told me she had decided to turn them over to the Department of Children and Family Services the next Monday. If she had done so, they would have been in the system, and I would have always thought they were with my wife. They would have been lost to me forever.

At that moment I made up my mind that they'd never be away from me again, and I stayed true to that vow until they were adults.

It was clearly God who led me to my children. I would not have thought about that babysitter, would not have gone there at all, had I not had a constant impulse that got stronger until I was guided to them. I'll always have faith in God.

"It was as if I had forgotten something"

JAMES MATEKA, *Construction Manager*

I t was November 20, 1971, and I was a sophomore at the University of Albuquerque. I was off-campus attending a party when I got a sensation, or a calling—like an instinct—to go back to the campus dormitory. It was as if I had forgotten something, like the way you feel when you're not sure whether you left the house unlocked. I left the party and went back to the dorm. As I entered the dorm lobby and headed toward my room, I walked past a bank of twelve to fifteen pay telephones. One was ringing and for absolutely no reason I picked it up. It was my father calling from Chicago to tell me my grandmother had died.

I flew to Chicago the next morning to be with my family and attend the funeral.

I often think back on the odds of this happening, and I believe God intervened to give me a tap on the shoulder to leave the party and then to pick up a ringing telephone—which otherwise I never would have done.

"One second later and it would have been too late"

RON VANDERVALK, *Software Company Owner*

It was 1997 and I was working from home programming computer software. My son was six and my daughter five. My home office is adjacent to my bedroom and is separated by sliding doors. The kids were sitting on my bed watching TV and I was working on my computer. The doors were closed to keep out the sound of the TV.

About an hour or so passed and all of a sudden, for no reason at all, I stopped typing midsentence and got up to check on the kids. It was the weirdest thing. When I opened the sliding doors, my heart fell into my stomach. I screamed out, "*Stop!*" My daughter was standing on the corner of the bed facing my son, and his arms were back and about to push her off.

She was lined up exactly with the corner of the bureau, and based on her height and distance from where she was standing, she would have gone backward and hit her head on the corner of the furniture with tragic results.

I almost don't believe it when I think back about what happened. I can't explain it. I'm not a particularly religious person, but I believe with all my heart that God touched me that day and made me get up and go into the bedroom. I was busy working and there was absolutely no reason at all for me to stop, midsentence, to check on my kids. The fact that I opened the door just as my son was about to push my daughter is too much of a coincidence to be anything else. One second later and it would have been too late.

"I thank God for giving me that feeling"

BETTE LU FORSYTHE, *Retired Pharmacist*

In October 1997 I went to my family physician, Dr. Trevino ("Dr. T") for my yearly physical. He ran a series of routine blood tests. I requested a chest X-ray because I remember thinking I hadn't had one in many years. Dr. T asked, "Do you have any symptoms?" "No," I said. He made it clear to me that unless I had specific symptoms, the procedure wouldn't be covered by insurance. Despite his saying this, some feeling I had insisted that I get it done and pay for it myself.

The following week, Dr. T called me with the X-ray report. It revealed a shadow on one of my lungs. Further tests revealed a possible lung cancer. After a series of exams by specialists, I was operated on. One lobe was removed, and that dark area was found to be cancer.

Later, three different specialists asked me how I knew to get the X-ray. I couldn't give them an answer. It was a feeling I couldn't explain. I thank God for giving me that feeling. Why did I listen? I don't know. I'm just an ordinary person. I believe that if people are sensitive and listen, they will get messages and their lives will change. The experience confirmed to me a power beyond us.

"I have something to tell you"

DONNA ORCHARD, *School Teacher/Administrator*

In the fall of 1998, while driving home from an afternoon movie, my nineteen-year-old son began to shake, his white knuckles tightening on the steering wheel. Our lighthearted mood suddenly changed when he said, "Hey guys, I have something to tell you." "Okay," his stepdad said as we nodded our heads. My son looked over his shoulder at us and said, "I'm gay."

I looked at my beautiful son, now on the dean's list as he worked his way through college as a tenor section leader in an Episcopal church. My response, I suspect, was typical. I cried the way he had cried in the mall when he looked up at me after discovering there was no Santa. I squalled about AIDS and about not having grandchildren. My mind raced: "Will my son be relegated to singles bars and multiple partners and never find love? What if he steps into the wrong bar in Alabama?" I wrestled with God: "Life is hard enough without this! My beautiful son is tender and warm and knows nothing of violence. How can I protect him? Will he be treated fairly on a job or be fired if his boss finds out? Will he have to live far away from me in San Francisco or New York to be safer? Will we be separated by miles and also by a lifestyle I don't understand? God, how could you do this?" I was raised a traditional Baptist—to have a gay son wasn't in the plan!

Thirty minutes later we got out of the car, and I reached for my son and we hugged. At that moment, my body relaxed into

God's perfect peace. "Benjamin," I said, "there's nothing you could tell me that would make me love my boy any less."

I went from the typical mother reaction—"Life is hard enough without this"—to thinking thirty minutes later, "Well, of course Benjamin is gay." I felt God's presence throughout that whole conversation.

I personally believe it is my Higher Power—which I call God—who intervened and allowed me to see this all as a blessing. Today I can't imagine my son *not* being gay!

"She never regained consciousness"

RON SKARBO, *Retail Furniture Business Owner*

I n late November 1996 I decided to do something I'd never done before—fly to Palm Springs from Seattle just for the weekend, to watch a golf tournament. The idea was so out of character for me that I'm sure my wife thought I'd lost my mind when I suggested it. We didn't do things like that. It was too spur-of-the-moment. But we went.

My wife and I and our youngest son flew to Palm Springs to watch an annual professional tournament called the Skins Game. My parents had a winter home in the area, so we surprised them when we showed up at their house on Saturday night. As excited as they were, they were also disappointed we hadn't planned to spend more time with them. So we offered to take them to dinner the next night following the golf tournament. We made a date to meet at 6 p.m.

The tournament ran late, and by the time we got to my parents' it was almost eight o'clock and they'd already eaten dinner. I apologized for standing them up and gave our excuses, but it seemed that no matter what I said, I wasn't getting through to Mom. She was clearly miffed. As the evening wore on, I did everything I could think of to break her mood. My repeated apologies and her apparent reluctance to accept them eventually became kind of funny. Finally I stood in front of her, took her face in my hands, stared into her eyes, kissed her, told her how sorry I was to have missed our date, and then told her I loved her. Finally she let it go and laughed with the rest of us at her stubbornness.

We flew home the next morning and I was back in my office by noon. An hour later I got a call from Dad. He told me that Mom had suffered an aneurysm and was in the hospital and unconscious.

I flew back to Palm Springs that afternoon and spent the rest of the week with Dad, visiting Mom in the hospital. She never regained consciousness and passed away.

For whatever reason, I spent the last evening of my mother's conscious life speaking sweetly to her, looking into her eyes, kissing her, and telling her I loved her. There has never been a doubt in my mind that this was a wonderful gift from God.

"I was now a hostage"

JORDAN RICH, *Radio Broadcaster*

I've been an admirer of God's work all my life. One dramatic incident reminds me of the strength of my relationship with him.

The year was 1992, the month October. It was a crisp autumn day in New England. I ended my morning-drive radio shift at an FM Boston music station and headed for a nearby stereo store to pick up a repaired amplifier. It was about 10:30 in the morning, smack-dab in the heart of a busy suburban downtown shopping plaza. I parked my Jeep in front of the store and strolled through the front door, my mind focused on all the other errands I needed to do that day.

I hadn't noticed the hooded man standing quietly against the storefront. As I walked in, he followed me and placed a shotgun at the nape of my neck. I felt the cold steel of the gun and listened to his curse-laden commands to behave. We then came upon his three accomplices, who were already threatening the store's owners.

The owners were bound and placed on their knees facing the floor. I was told, in no uncertain terms, not to move or I'd "be blown away." I was now a hostage. The robbers took my wallet and keys and forced me up a short flight of stairs to a closet area, where I was told not to move.

It seemed surreal, of course. I had walked straight into an armed robbery in progress—here in the middle of a bright and sunny morning. I thought of how unnecessary and stupid it would be to lose my life for something as silly as a power amplifier.

As I contemplated my life, I thought of my wife, Wendy, who was eight months' pregnant with our second child. All I could think about was the baby I might not live to see. I prayed hard, and as I did, I experienced a sense of calm. God seemed to surround me in the closet. A voice in my head kept repeating that I was going to be fine and not to worry. The voice felt like my own, but it had a confidence and sureness that could only have come from a greater power. That voice kept me from panicking and allowed me to breathe and relax during the thirty minutes I was being threatened and bullied by the thugs.

The robbers fled the store with a small amount of cash and a few stereo parts. I walked away from that scary experience knowing without question that God had other plans for me. I was not meant to die there that day. There would be a lot of life, love, and learning to come.

I got a tap on the shoulder from him shortly thereafter. His sense of timing was impeccable. It was one month after the robbery. I was in the maternity ward having just watched the birth of my son Andrew when my phone rang. It was the district attorney's office calling to tell me they had just apprehended the four robbery suspects.

I looked up and thanked God for helping the good guys crack the case and for being by my side during the robbery. He was there with me the day they threatened my life, just as he was at that glorious moment Andrew came into the world. I'm a lucky man.

"It was now or never"

In January 1992 I was a theological student and had been living with Amanda for three years. She was clear about her feelings. She wished to move forward and get married and then pregnant. I was forty-nine and she was thirty-four. I had gone through a painful divorce four years earlier, and I wasn't ready to commit again. After I had set and then postponed three wedding dates, Amanda took a stand. It was now or never.

I was very distressed. It felt impossible to go in either direction. So I did what I frequently do when I'm distressed and confused—I went to pray. I took my old camping van and drove to a park near our home in Colorado.

Amanda had given me a Lakota peace pipe. In the Native American tradition, a loved one who best knows your spirit gives it to you. After I received it, a friend who is a Lakota medicine man instructed me in the responsibilities that came with the pipe. He told me that by accepting the pipe I was agreeing to walk in peace, to set aside acting in anger, and to act with compassion toward others. I took the responsibilities very seriously.

It was one of those January days that happens only occasionally in the western United States—it was sunny and warm. I scooted to the very edge of the opening of the sliding door of the van to be as much in the warm sun as I could. I was facing the mountains and began the ritual of praying with the peace pipe.

As I did, two bald eagles appeared far up in the sky. They

were obviously mates. They slowly circled closer and closer until finally they were circling overhead, less than a hundred feet from me. I knew, immediately and completely, why the eagles were there and what I was supposed to do with this blessing. I knew at that moment I was being touched by God. I had been immersed in ambivalence about moving forward with marriage. In an instant, that ambivalence was replaced with absolute clarity.

After a minute or so of circling, the pair began to lift back up. They hit the thermals and were gone.

I quickly finished the ritual, drove home like a bat out of hell, ran into the house, and told Amanda it was time to get married.

Three weeks later, our friend the Lakota medicine man and a Unitarian Universalist minister joined us.

Our daughter, Hannah Joy, was born January 12, 1994, and we recently celebrated our fifteenth wedding anniversary. It is a good life!

"My thoughts were literally bombarded"

CARLA CAMERON, *Photographer*

I was at a stage in my life when I wondered if God had forgotten me. I had been asking God for the gift of healing and I wasn't getting it. It was an unanswered prayer and I didn't understand why.

It was just after Thanksgiving and I was making a turkey sandwich when my son, who was just under a year old, started fussing at me. I handed him a little piece of bread and continued making my sandwich. Piece by piece I put the turkey on the bread. When I looked over at him, he was staring at the turkey. I knew that's what he wanted, but there was no way he could chew meat. So instead of giving him the turkey, I gave him a little piece of cookie to make up for it—I knew this would do the trick. But much to my surprise, it didn't. I looked at him and saw the bread squished in one hand and the cookie completely crumbled in the other. He wanted that turkey and he began to cry.

I was so frustrated for him. I knew how much he wanted the meat, but he could choke on it. There was no way he could have it.

And then it hit me. My thoughts were literally bombarded. It was almost as if I was tuning into God's radio station—tuning into his frequency. God caught my attention mentally and spoke to my heart. He said, "Carla, you're no different, my child. I have given you my word, and it was not enough. Then I started revealing the many talents and gifts I chose just for you, and you discarded them as if they had no value. Please understand, the very thing you're mad at me for not giving to you now will choke you."

I looked at my son and thought, "This must be how God feels when one of his kids is asking for something and he can't give it to them." It was a life lesson for me. It allowed me to see that there are some things I'm not ready for. From that day on, I realized that God had not forgotten me, and that out of love he protected me. It's not that he didn't want to give me the desire of my heart—I wasn't mature enough to handle what I was asking for. I now believe God doesn't withhold any good thing from us unless it's for our own protection. His timing is perfect!

"The communication was more like thought waves"

MOSHE BERNSTEIN, *Rabbi/Writer*

My heartbeat accelerated as the brown leather satchel passed through the X-ray screener at the San Francisco International Airport. Despite my nervousness, I knew rationally that the machine would not register the object of power contained in that bag: a three-hundred-year-old handwritten Hebrew manuscript.

The story behind the book was, in itself, miraculous. Just a few months before, in late August 2002, a volunteer worker at the New Norcia Monastery north of Perth, Australia, had discovered the manuscript wrapped in butcher paper on a shelf in the monastery's library. It had never been cataloged.

The reason the manuscript was now in my possession had to do with its content: kabbalah. The study of Jewish mysticism is one of my lifetime passions. Because of my reputation as a teacher and lecturer on the subject, the abbot of the monastery had contacted me to verify the book's authenticity.

I traveled to New Norcia with three rabbinical colleagues to examine the text. Once I had seen the book, a veritable treasure of Jewish culture, I became obsessed with reclaiming it for the Jewish people. The book was one of seventeen handwritten copies of the *Shoshan Sodot,* the original of which dated back to 1495. It was a compendium of all the kabbalistic wisdom that had emerged up until that time. *Shoshan Sodot* translates to "Lily of Mysteries." However, in Jewish numerology, the word *Shoshan* had the numerical value of 656—thus the book's title was also "Six Hundred Fifty-Six Mysteries." All six hundred fifty-six of its mysteries, including meditative visualizations, astrological charts, and magical incantations, were intact. Its discovery in a monastery in the remote bush of Western Australia was for me, as a kabbalist, comparable to a jeweler's finding a superlative diamond in some obscure alleyway.

Though the book might have been a valuable asset for the cash-strapped monastery, there was no financial transaction involved; it was given freely and altruistically. Thus began for me an eight-week journey across the globe together with this distinctive artifact, with the aim of searching for a repository appropriate to its cultural, historical, and monetary value.

As the satchel emerged from the other end of the detector in San Francisco, I breathed a silent sigh of relief. After I had strapped it over my shoulder, my wife and I made our way to the gate where our flight to the East Coast was boarding.

We spent a week visiting my parents in Philadelphia, including Christmas Day, on which we celebrated their fifty-first wedding anniversary. Although, like most Jewish people, they did not have a great understanding or appreciation of kabbalah, they were impressed with the significance of the unique text I carried with me.

From Philadelphia we drove to West Orange, New Jersey, to spend some time with my sister and her two girls.

On December 31 we were scheduled to fly to New Orleans on free airline tickets for three days. I had originally planned to take the manuscript with me, as it had become an almost inseparable companion from the time the abbot had placed it in my hands.

My sister, however, convinced me it would be much safer in her suburban home while we traveled.

The home had a large basement that had been converted into guests accommodations. After we had packed our carry-on luggage with the outfits we would need for our brief excursion to New Orleans, I took the manuscript, placed it carefully inside my larger suitcase, which lay flat on the basement floor, and then locked it for added security.

The taxi to the airport was due any minute. I walked up the basement stairs with my carry-on luggage, but at the top of the stairs I stopped dead in my tracks. Unmistakably, the book was communicating to me. It is difficult to describe, as the communication was more like thought waves than audible words. Nevertheless, the message was clear: the book was not happy being left there in the suitcase.

I quickly descended the stairs, unlocked the suitcase, and pulled out the brown leather satchel. Looking hastily around the room, I opened the door of a small broom closet and placed the bag inside, on one of the upper shelves. I once again ascended the stairs. The taxi was already waiting for us in front of the house.

On the way to the airport I thought about what I had done—based only on an irrational voice inside my head. Why had I removed this valuable manuscript from a locked suitcase and left it, unsecured, on an open shelf? Was I a total idiot or simply insane?

New Year's Eve in New Orleans was a wild and wondrous affair. Not being a drinker, I felt very much an outsider to the frenzied celebrations. Nevertheless, in the background of the picturesque French Quarter, bombarded with the raucous, rhythmic beat of competing bands, it was a memorable event.

The next morning we were awakened by a telephone call from my distraught sister. During the night, her basement had flooded. Both of our suitcases and all their contents had been completely submerged. The only item that had escaped inundation was the kabbalistic manuscript.

"I'M NOT READY TO GO"

Coming Back from the Other Side

"I'm not ready to go"

JANE SEYMOUR, *Actress/Entrepreneur*

I was filming *The Onassis Story* in Spain and had a bad bronchitis infection. A doctor was brought to the set and I was given an injection of antibiotics. Immediately I knew something was wrong. I felt as if my throat was closing. I tried to speak up but couldn't.

The next thing I remember, I was panicking and then I wasn't panicking. I was very calm, but I wasn't. I was looking down at my body. I saw this man screaming—yelling, *"Emergency! Emergency!"* I was now rolled over—I was half-naked. I had two huge syringes in my backside, and I was watching from the corner of the room. And I saw this white light. I had no pain. I had no tension. I just kind of looked and thought, "That's very strange. That's me. But that can't be me if I'm here." Then I realized I was out of my body and that I was going to die.

All of a sudden I just looked, and I said, "No, no, I'm not ready to go away. I want to get back in that body. I have children I want to raise and there's so much I want to do. I want to give back, I want to do so much in the world, and I'm just, I'm not ready to go."

So I asked whoever was up there—God, a Higher Power, whatever one wants to call it—I just said, "Whoever you are, I will never deny your existence, just please let me back in that body and I won't let you down. I will never let you down. I'm not going to waste one minute of my life if I have it back." The next thing I knew, I was in my body.

I believe there is some spiritual entity that's greater than us. I have always believed that and I believe it even more so now. I believe someone is listening to me and is giving me an incredibly blessed life.

"I went into full cardiac arrest and was pronounced dead"

KATHY BAKER, *Security Company Owner*

I t was May 16, 1985, and I was admitted to the hospital for a very routine event, to give birth. After nineteen hours of unsuccessful labor, the doctors decided to do a C-section. I happened to work as a nurse on that floor of the hospital and had total confidence in this decision and the people making it. I knew everything would be okay.

After fifteen minutes in the operating room, the doctors were ready to take the baby, but a problem developed. The epidural anesthetic had accidentally been injected into my veins. At 8:17 p.m. my daughter was born, and at the same moment my heart stopped beating. I felt myself suffocating. I went into full cardiac arrest and was pronounced dead.

I watched the crash team come in to resuscitate me. I watched as the doctor screamed to the anesthesiologist, *"How much time? How much time?"*

As I hovered above my body on the operating table, a very loving being that I call God spoke to me and told me I would be fine and to go to the light. I remember I was communicating, not by mouth, but through my mind. I then remember turning upward and going up a tunnel in what I would describe as a g-force. There were no hands on me.

As I went through the tunnel, I passed other beings who gave me an incredible sense of love. I neared the top and entered a bright light that didn't hurt my eyes. I passed through the light and came upon a beautiful road. From the road I was led to a building, and when I entered it, there were beautiful lights of all different colors everywhere around me.

I was then met by some very loving beings who told me of things to come in my life. They explained to me that life is very simple and that we complicate it with problems. They told me we are meant to learn to love ourselves, and then others. They said the hardest lesson is to learn how to love ourselves first. They said people mistake this love for selfishness and think that loving other people is the real lesson. But, they said, that way of thinking often causes confusion and problems. They said we couldn't accept others for who they are if we haven't accepted ourselves first.

These beings went on to tell me there are many lessons we are supposed to learn here and that lessons will come in many forms. They said that what we perceive as a negative lesson is actually a positive one—for our growth. I was then told I had to go back. I remember telling them I wanted to stay.

I was in a semicoma for three days. When I woke, I told the doctors and nurses what I had seen them doing and heard them saying when I was in the operating room. They confirmed my experience for me when they said, "There's no way you could've known that. You were flatlined!"

After arriving home, I couldn't speak about this experience for many years, but I hold close to me the love and guidance God gave me. I know God sent me back to help others see the beauty and light instead of darkness.

"I no longer fear death or, in fact, fear anything"

JANICE LUNNON, *Aged Care Field Officer*

In January 1995 I traveled to New Zealand with a group called the Foundation of Higher Learning to attend a two-week silent Zen retreat. This group meets to learn the ancient teachings of different religions. On this particular retreat we were meditating and chanting in hopes of raising our vibration spiritually, to become better and more loving people. Our goal was to raise human consciousness to a higher plane of peace and love and, by doing so, to raise spiritual awareness globally.

A few days after the retreat, I sat down at home to meditate by myself. I had just dropped into a really deep, peaceful state where my thoughts had finally stopped buzzing around my head when I suddenly felt as if I was floating up into the air. Amazed, I looked down and realized that it wasn't my body that had risen, but another part of myself. I was in a blissful state, looking down at my body. I remember thinking, and feeling uncomfortable. I didn't know where I was going or if I'd be able to stop the experience. I watched from above until panic took hold of me and I floated back into my body.

I was incredibly excited afterward because I realized I had just proven to myself that I was a soul and was separate from my physical self. I haven't looked back since and have never doubted again that I am an eternal, reincarnating soul. Now I no longer fear death or, in fact, fear anything.

"Save the children"

HERBERT SEE POY, *Jazz Musician*

Early in the morning on May 15, 2005, my friend Pedro and I set out from Cairns (North Queensland, Australia) to Innisfail with Pedro's six-meter fiberglass boat in tow. We launched the boat at the mouth of the Johnstone River and headed for Howie Reef, part of the famous Great Barrier Reef.

As soon as we threw our lines in, the fish were on the bite. It wasn't long before we had to stop to clean and ice down what we had caught. By 7 p.m. we had caught our legal quota and our icebox was full to the brim. We had a bite to eat and were in very high spirits. Our original intention was to stay overnight, but we decided to surprise our families and go home early.

Navigation was not a problem as we had a GPS (global positioning system), but on reaching the mouth of the river we were unable to see the red light buoy. The buoy is the marker that safely guides boaters through a narrow passage, past dangerous rocks, and into the river. To make things worse, there was a very heavy fog. We found out later that the light on the buoy was not operational that night.

I was driving the boat and Pedro was sitting on the bow looking for the buoy when it happened. We hit the very rocks we were trying to avoid! Pedro was thrown twenty feet onto the rocks, and I was thrown forward into the steering wheel and dashboard. I remember ringing 000 (911) on my mobile phone and giving details. I don't remember scaling the oyster-covered rocks that gashed my left leg and severed two tendons in my ankle and shin. Police later told my son they found me staggering down the road.

The noise of the rescue helicopter woke me briefly, but I don't remember arriving in Cairns, or anything else for the next five weeks while I was in an induced coma at the Cairns Base Hospital intensive care unit.

During those five weeks, suffering from punctured and collapsed lungs, six broken ribs, and gashes on my legs and chin, I contracted pneumonia several times. The fourth time, conventional treatment was no longer working. Doctors told my close friend Greta that I was in a critical state and they were not hopeful I would recover. Before leaving home that morning she prayed on the telephone with my lifelong friend Bishop George Tung Yep.

When Greta arrived at the hospital, she was immediately admitted to my side. She sat down, held my hand, and repeated the prayer she had said with Bishop Tung Yep. As she prayed, a nurse came into the room and introduced herself. She said her name was Sue and told Greta she was assisting a doctor who was conducting human trials of a new drug that worked to fight against multiple infections and viruses. She asked Greta if she would consider allowing her to test the drug on me.

I was now on full life support and was going downhill fast. The nurse explained that it was the very last day any new person could be admitted to the trials. She would have to e-mail and fax the pharmaceutical company in the United States by early afternoon to make it happen.

My family gave the go-ahead. Miraculously, I was out of danger within twelve hours of the start of treatment. Two weeks later, when my lungs were functioning without life support, I was brought out of the coma.

The first thing I did was beckon for a pen and paper. These

are the words I wrote: "I have been to heaven and spoken to God. I have to save the children."

My recollection of heaven started with a barbecue beside a crystal-clear stream overhung with beautiful, pristine trees. I said to the person I was with, "What are we going to eat? We have not brought any food." He said, "What would you like?" And I replied, "Prawns would be nice." He took a net and dipped it into the water and it came out full of prawns.

I then walked down a pathway that led to a stone wall about three feet high by three feet wide and three feet deep. It was dark, and on passing through the entrance I came into a huge valley surrounded by mountains. At that very moment every mountain exploded into the most spectacular fireworks display I have ever seen. Huge glowing boulders were being thrown high into the air, but no one got hurt. In the glittering light I could see thousands of people and they were having a hedgehog barbecue! The noise was deafening and the flashes of light were blinding. It was something that couldn't be experienced on Earth.

When the noise stopped, I saw the back of a man in a long white robe walking among the people some distance from where I was sitting. I called to him, "Is that you, God?" He did not answer. Then I said, "What is all this noise and hullabaloo about?" The voice that replied filled the entire universe: "Save the children. Spend all your time, all your energy, and all your money on saving the children. Never let there be another sick, hungry, or unhappy child."

The voice did not speak again, and on closer observation I noticed that the entire crowd of thousands was made up of children from about six to twelve years old. I believe it was Jesus I called out to, but it was God's voice that answered.

I had a religious upbringing and have always been a believer. If I had any doubt before, this experience strengthened my belief in the hereafter and put the final stamp of approval on my faith.

Since the accident I have found a new zest for my music. I'm putting all my energy and time into practicing my saxophone and writing new songs. I'm hoping to record a CD of this music to benefit a charity for children.

"Perpetual euphoria"

JENNIFER SKIFF, *Journalist/Author*

It was my twelfth birthday and I was given a brand-new ten-speed bicycle. Along with the bike, my mother gave strict instructions not to under any circumstances ride on a nearby busy road called Route 102. But with the urging of a friend I was soon gliding along 102.

All of a sudden I felt the most wonderful feeling—the only way to describe it would be to say it was like perpetual euphoria. I looked down. Below me about thirty feet was a Volkswagen Bug. In its cracked windshield was something that looked like a blond wig. A crumpled body was curled up on the pavement in front of the car.

I watched as two women got out of the VW and went to the body. Other cars stopped and people rushed to help. I saw my friend, frozen in fear, still holding her handlebars tightly. It was then that I realized the body was mine.

And then, in an instant, the wonderful sensation I was having vanished and I was back in my bloodied body, my head scalped and my spinal cord exposed.

A month later, I had fully recovered. But I never told anyone what really happened to me that day until I was an adult and heard that other people had had similar experiences. Since that day, I have never feared death.

"All religion is of man, not God"

STEVE SIRBACK, *Retired Deputy Sheriff*

On March 9, 2001, after having had two massive heart attacks, I underwent open-heart surgery for a quadruple bypass. After the surgery was completed, the surgeon was unable to restart my heart and I was clinically dead for approximately twenty minutes.

It was during this time that I passed through a tunnel of light and went to the other side of it. It was extremely beautiful there, with incredibly vibrant colors like nothing I had ever seen, and the sense of warmth, peace, and love I experienced was beyond description. I felt I was in the presence of something great, which I will call the Spirit of Light. It made me feel very humbled and loved.

This Spirit told me there are many truths that the world is not ready to accept and it is not yet time for these truths to be revealed. I was told that if I chose to return that I must deliver the following message:

> All religion is of man, not God. Religion separates us, and God wants us to be as one family, to worship him, the one and only God. To spend eternity in paradise, we must love God with all our heart and soul. But we must do much more than that. We must love, respect, forgive, and help one another. We must not judge others. We must never turn away from someone in need. We must love and respect all life—

yes, every living creature. If they did not have value, God would not have given them life. If mankind will do these things, then the world can and will survive, and we shall see paradise. If man continues to turn away from God, then man will pay for his disobedience.

The experience I had changed me and my life. I'm a much more caring person now. My goal is to relay this message to as many people as I can and in doing so, to bring more people to God and to the knowledge of how important it is to love one another.

Acknowledgments

THIS JOURNEY STARTED with a layover in San Diego while flying between Australia and New England. I had two glorious days to spend with one of my best friends. When my sister Katy asked me to have lunch with a friend of hers, I told her I didn't have time. But as luck (or intervention) would have it, I picked up one of those "I'm going to die any minute" nightmare flus on the flight from Sydney and was forced to extend my stay. When I felt better, I sat down to lunch with Katy's friend the Reverend Millie Landis. That's when Millie asked me if I had a "God Story," and with that one question, she passed the torch. Being around Millie is like capturing a moment with an angel. She has given me a beautiful gift.

My great friends and writing mentors, the hilarious Susan Maushart and the fascinating Elisabeth Luard, agreed it was a great idea for a book. So Elisabeth, to whom I am forever grateful, took my hand and put it into that of Abner Steins. Abner blanketed me in the safety of the outrageously special Susan Raihofer, who guided me through the writing of the sixty-page book proposal and into the arms of Julia Pastore, who "got it" immediately.

My glorious friends did as they always have—sustained and encouraged me. Carolyn O'Neil is a wealth of knowledge and has supported my every endeavor with great enthusiasm. The amazing Becky Madeira sprang to action with her publicity skills, and my awe-inspiring brother Jim Skiff put up the website, GodStories.com. Jess Loo and Anna Bradley—fabulous, compassionate women—helped with the research.

For a lifetime of love and support, I give thanks to Crystal Canney, Janet Field-Back, Laura Gower, and Beth Jackson. For showering me with acts of kindness during this project, I am grateful to Sara Baer-Sinnott and K. Dun Gifford, Amy Bennett, Chrissie Brown, Sandi Brown, Rosemary Canney, Susannah Carr, Lisa Castaldo, Katie Chapman, Grant Castle, Patti Chapman, Amy Clemons, Susan and David Rockefeller, Mara Craig, Nancy Dawson, Catherine Fleay, Joan Galos, Ita Goldberger, Stephen and Rogina Jeffries, Steve "Cosmo" Kassels, Michele "Splendiferous" LaFond, Dianne "always positive" Laurance, Liz and Arthur Martinez, Jacqueline Montfort, Douglas Munro, Genie Murray, Anne and Bruce "Cupcake" Pomeroy, Kathy Shields, Adam Sigel, Ali Thompson, Carole Tomko-Recka, Marisa Tribe, and Bo Wisniewski.

To the women I swim with in the ocean in Australia and on the lake in Maine, thank you for your ability to swim and laugh at the same time. To the good people working to help animals throughout the world that I've come to call friends, thank you for your passion, which fuels my own. To Ted Turner, for providing me with a lifetime of opportunity, and to Jane Seymour, who graciously shared her story and gave this book wings, thank you for your kindheartedness.

The media embraced the concept of "God Stories" and gave this project life. The following people and their support teams played an important role in making it all happen: Earl Brechlin, Jeff Brucculeri, Ann Charles, Kate Daniels, Gary Dickson, Dave Durian, Hec Gauthier, Jonathon Gifford, Bob Gourley, Rosemary Greenham, Allan Handelman, Jack Harris, Judy Harrison,

Pat Hernandez, Annie Jennings, Dennis Kelly, Natalie Knox, Nicholas Kratsas, Don Lancer, Lars Larson, Deborah Leavitt, Matthew Lymbury, G. Jeffrey MacDonald, Keith McDonald, Geraldine Mellet, Brenda Michaels, Leslie Miller, Mark Miller, Mike Moran, Luke Morfesse, Jordan Rich, Don Russel, Monty Sangar, Jim Scott, Fiona Sewell, Bev Smith, Rob Spears, Will Sterling, Brad Storey, Sharon Taylor, Shawn Taylor, Richard Walburg, Tedd Webb, and Bernadette Young.

It has been extremely satisfying to work with my very own team of consummate professionals at Harmony Books. I've never had so much fun working with editors in my life! My respect and thanks go to Shaye Areheart and everyone at Harmony, Crown, and Random House who made this project their own.

I am grateful to have three parents who are proud of their children, who love them and have raised them without expectations and free of hate. I thank my wonderful father for his sense of humor and his unconditional and supportive love every day of my life.

My sisters and brothers are beautiful souls. Thanks to Katy for her generosity, to Billy for always giving sound advice, to Jimmy for always being there for me, and to Sarah and Lisa, my magnificent little sisters. Thank you for always laughing at me. There is no laughter better than when it's shared with you—even when the joke's on me. To my family in Australia, especially my Wren, thank you for bringing so much light into my life.

My dogs are my constant joy. I thank Couscous and Chickpea, who have shown me that to write a good book, you must go for a walk at least four times a day.

To my own James Bond, Jon: thank you for searching the world, finding me, and then taking me by the hand and showing me life's a party. You are all things wonderful, my lovely man. Thank you for warming my heart and keeping me safe. I adore you.

To have a God Story is to have been given the greatest gift of all, confirmation that there is more. Nearly every person who submitted a story for this book told me they felt called to share it. I believe we were all brought together for a reason and it's a big one! I consider the journey ours.

About the Author

JENNIFER SKIFF'S AWARD-WINNING career as an international television journalist includes more than a decade as an investigative correspondent for CNN. Her specialty is the environment, and among other industry honors she has received the prestigious Environmental Media Award. Passionate about animals and their welfare, she works with charities throughout the world to bring relief to abused and abandoned animals.

A cancer scare in her early thirties convinced Jennifer that a Divine presence was active in her life. Her journalistic instincts took over, and she began a quest to find out if others had similar experiences. The result is her first book, *God Stories*, a collection of inspiring first-person accounts of miracle-like encounters with God.

With her husband and dogs, Jennifer spends her life in perpetual summer between Maine and Australia.

To find out more and to share your own God Story, visit www.GodStories.com.